Give Yourself Permission To Be Phenomenal

By Discovering Your Purpose!

With The Love, Support, And Power of A Partnership

7-Weeks to Your Phenomenal Purpose

Author Carolyn McCall

AuthorHouse™
1663 Liberty Drive
Bloomington, IN 47403
www.authorhouse.com
Phone: 833-262-8899

This book is printed on acid-free paper.

ISBN: 979-8-8230-0590-6 (sc)
ISBN: 979-8-8230-0592-0 (hc)
ISBN: 979-8-8230-0591-3 (e)

Library of Congress Control Number: 2023906768

Print information available on the last page.

Published by AuthorHouse 07/02/2024

authorHOUSE®

Contents

Trust The Process

Preface

TO THE READER

Carolyn McCall want you to know that - every exercise and every activity requested of you in this book, we have experienced ourselves, and each story in the book happened. If not for these exercises and activities, which taught us the most about ourselves. This book would not have been possible. Our life experiences, particularly the painful ones, often serve as a catalyst for personal growth and self-discovery. Many people fail to recognize that unfortunate and tragic circumstances and situations provide a window into our life's purpose. When we understand the lessons these traumatic and sometimes life-altering situations come to teach. We find the strength to translate our experiences into inspired change. This change removes the veil clouding our perception to reestablish who we are and what we are meant to do in our lives, which is how we break free from the old patterns of insecurity, lack, and heartache. These experiences lead us to our purpose if we are willing to take the journey inside ourselves.

Jesus, from the Gnostic Gospel of Thomas, said, "If you bring forth that which is within you, then that which is within you will be your salvation. If you do not bring forth that which is within you, then that which is within you will destroy you." Jesus's quote encapsulates the inherent power of *self-discovery* and its potential consequences. Throughout this seven-week process, be willing to discover *what is within you* that wants to emerge for you to live your purpose. This process is about gaining clarity, insight, and new awareness and removing the obstacles, challenges, and barriers that keep you stuck in complacency, self-importance, egotism, and pompous attitudes. The metaphorical veil that shrouds our minds can prevent us from hearing the gentle whispers of our inner voice. This voice is our purpose, calling us to permit ourselves to be phenomenal by living in our purpose.

Neglecting this inner voice and failing to express ourselves led to internal strife, emotional stagnation, and social regression for the whole world. When we tune in to our inner voice, we can unlock the wisdom and guidance within. Only then can we embark on a journey of authenticity and fulfillment? *Enjoy this journey!*

IT WILL BE LIFE-CHANGING IF YOU TRUST THE PROCESS.

Acknowledgment

At a young age, my mother instilled in me the belief that I have a unique purpose in life and that it is my responsibility to pursue it wholeheartedly. I owe much of my readiness to write this book to her example of courage and determination. She has an unwavering belief in me and constantly reminds me that I can achieve greatness by trusting God and acting on his word. *Thank you,* Mom, for always believing in me and showing me what Faith, Hope, and Love look like daily. *I Love You* from the moon and back!

My Co-Authors Debra Lynn Carter and Cheryl McConnell (My Sisters)

Thank you, sisters, for reshaping my perspective and providing phenomenal awareness throughout my writing journey. Your wisdom, insight, and constructive feedback were invaluable. It helped me break free from the chains of self-doubt, fear, and worry, permitting me to embrace the transformative power within us all. I am so BLESSED to have each of you as a sister. *"Thank you both!"*

Specifically, to my sister Debra Lynn Carter, *"Thank you"* for being my older sister. You are a *wise sage* and a pillar of strength for our family. I wouldn't be on this journey if you hadn't taught me how to call on Jesus by "Get on my knees and pray to God" during a moment in my life when my world was crumbling all around me. Thank you for always Trusting God and showing me what "Faithfulness" looks like. Your resiliency has been a guiding light for me and your brilliant son, Brian Lee Dixon, who is like my son and one of the strongest people I know. He is the *"Truth Teller" and a fantastic* human being. *Brian, thank you for being the son I never had. Your LOVE has been so fulfilling in my life! I love you with all my heart for filling that void! Deb, I love you for being a great example!*

To my Twin-Sister Cheryl McConnell, WOW! There is something magical about being a twin. When two souls are born together, a bond is created instantly. I came into the world with you, and you gave me unwavering support, unconditional love, and constant encouragement that shaped who I am today. When I think of you, I hear a quote that you always say to me, *"You Do YOU!"* Each of your children, LaToyna, La Shanda, Alicia, and Mack, are "Blessed" to have a mother with a heart and soul that Loves so profoundly. *I love you, twin!*

To my eldest brother, David Allen McCall, *"Thank you"* for calling me weekly to say, *"I Love You!"* That has meant more to me than you will ever know. Another "Blessing" I have received from you is your ability to be satisfied with the small things. You have taught me that it's not about things. It's about the people you love! *I Love You!* To my brother Robert Shawn McCall, what a GREAT example you have been to show what it looks like to dedicate your life to your son Hunter McCall. Moving from one state to another to be close enough to your son in college - is real dedication and self-sacrifice! Thank you for your Love and constant encouragement throughout my life. *Also, thank you, Tia, for being Hunter's determined, dedicated, and compassionate mother. I Love You ALL very much!*

To my brother Kristen Paul McCall, you are my third brother and another wonderful example of what a father will do to support his children. Madison, Maia, and Margo Rae McCall are lucky to have a dad like you. Your stable and consistent presence in their life has molded them into Amazing young adults. I *"Thank You"* for your dependability, brutal honesty, and love. Your endless Love and acceptance in my life have fostered a sense of belonging and emotional support. *I Love You and each of your children! Also, thank you, Rachel, for being a fantastic, strong, and wise mother to your children.* To my baby brother Stephen Merritt, I Love You! Your consistently calm presence, total love, and acceptance presence. Thank you for the balance you bring to our family. *I love you!*

I also want to "Thank" three women who have provided honest feedback and priceless recommendations during the progression of this book. Their expertise as corporate trainers and professional speakers offered me the insight - I needed to deepen my awareness of this journey. These women's names are Carolyn Nash-Edwards, La Shahn Taylor-Jackson, and Dr. TiCarol Smith. Ladies, I am forever indebted to you for your loving Faith and Inspiration. I Love You!

Last but certainly not least, I must *"Thank God."* I am immensely grateful for your unwavering gentleness and kindness in guiding me along this journey. Your Divine presence has been a soothing balm, comforting me during moments of confusion or uncertainty. Whether through your gentle whispers or subtle nudges, your wisdom has consistently been filled with compassion and understanding. You opened me up to new possibilities and insights that may have remained hidden. You helped me see beyond the surface and illuminated my path to manage the challenges and obstacles of writing a book. Thank you for your enlightenment, patience, reliability, and unfailing presence.

Introduction

Throughout the process of writing this book, I have come to realize what a humble and blessed experience it has been. Every step of the way, I have gained invaluable knowledge and insights that have shaped not only the content of this book but also my personal growth. The guidance and direction provided by God have been instrumental in helping me discover my potential as a writer and deepening my understanding of the subject matter. Looking back, I wouldn't change a thing for the knowledge I have gained. *This journey has taught me that incredible growth and transformation are possible when I allow God to lead m*e.

I wholeheartedly believe that embarking on the journey of co-creating with God through your purpose will be a blessing and a humbling experience. Bringing forth your purpose is sacred as you tap into the divine inspiration and guidance that flows through this journey. It is an opportunity to witness the beauty of collaboration between our human limitations and the infinite wisdom of God. As you surrender yourself to this creative process this journey takes you through, be willing to become a vessel through which profound messages and acts of your Divine purpose can be shared with the world.

I am grateful to you and eagerly anticipate the transformative experience that awaits you and your partner as you embark on this co-creative endeavor.

God Bless You,

Author Carolyn McCall

Three Sisters Story

Author
Carolyn McCall – BS, MA

Co-Author
Chaplain Debra L. Carter

Co-Author
Cheryl McConnell

Give Yourself Permission to be Phenomenal by Discovering Your Purpose was born in Kansas City, Missouri, during a class on cognitive psychology I taught in college. One of the critical components of this class was to create a safe and supportive learning environment for my students by encouraging them to question their negative self-perceptions and replace them with more positive and empowering ones to help them along their journey in college.

Witnessing my students' success in reshaping their thought patterns further reinforced the significance of partnerships and how they can serve as a catalyst for positive change. Recognizing the transformative power of education sparked a desire to partner with my eldest sister, Debra, and my twin sister, Cheryl. Through my newfound motivation, I decided to converse with my sisters during my eldest sister's (Debra) birthday party. The positive energy of that day filled the room with love, acceptance, and fresh perspectives. My sisters and I had no idea we were experiencing a rebirth in our relationship. This rebirth forged a sisterhood between us that inspired the significance of partnership and living our purpose as self-development coaches and facilitators.

When we joined forces, Debra and I created a dynamic workshop, and we invited my twin sister Cheryl to join us because of her expertise and insightfulness in emotional intelligence skills. With our collective wisdom, knowledge, and complex understanding of cognitive psychology and social cognitive behavior modification, we created effective learning environment in our workshops that cater to the unique needs of everyone participating. As we navigated the challenges and triumphs of these workshops, we realized that our aspirations go beyond personal fulfillment. We discovered that our calling is intricately connected to a higher purpose, a divine plan that involves developing minds. There isn't a more extraordinary experience than teaching people that they have the power to shape their minds, and inspire themselves to move forward. This unlocks one's true potential.

8

Section One:

In Section One, the book introduces key concepts that form the basis for subsequent exercises. These concepts are building blocks, enabling readers to work through the exercises with a solid understanding of the underlying principles. Explaining these fundamental concepts upfront ensures you know how to navigate the complexities outlined in section two.

Another crucial aspect of Section One is its emphasis on developing critical thinking skills. Through carefully crafted exercises, we encourage participants to their inner knowing, evaluate information critically, and form their perspectives. It empowers you to approach the journey with an insightful viewpoint.

Trust The Process

Section One
Part I:

Where To Start? Noah's Ark

During the pandemic, we all experienced a profound shift in perspective, in which a more purposeful life became undeniable as we witnessed the fragility of life and the interconnectedness of our global community. In the face of uncertainty and adversity, partnerships emerged as essential vehicles to fulfill one's purpose. Whether it was healthcare professionals working tirelessly on the frontlines or you volunteering to support vulnerable communities, partnerships became the driving force behind our collective pursuit of purpose.

During this time, I thought about Noah and the gravitational pull he must have felt when the *Divine* asked him to build an Ark. The pandemic and Noah's Ark share a common thread of unexpected challenges and the need for preparation. Noah's extraordinary Faith and obedience to God's command to build an ark without any sign of rain exemplify his unwavering Faith in God.

I am sure Noah's reaction to God's request could be described as a mixture of fear and obedience. The magnitude of the task at hand, constructing a massive vessel to withstand a catastrophic flood, would have undoubtedly caused Noah to feel uncertain. However, he recognized Faith and God's promise never to lead him astray. This belief overshadowed Noah's fear, leading him to embark on this monumental undertaking with determination and conviction. *What are you being asked to build or do?* To co-create with God, we must have Faith and allow ourselves to surrender to God's will. This way, we can become a positive catalyst for change.

Trust The Process

Section One
Part II:

The Importance of Partnership

Observing my twin sister and eldest sister's journey into motherhood has been a profound learning experience. Their dedication and commitment to raising their children through obstacles and adversities have shown me unwavering selflessness, unconditional love, and determination.

Therefore, the importance of partnership plays a crucial role along this journey. Truth and honesty in partnership help people identify and overcome the obstacles that hinder them in a partnership. When two people come together intending to support each other's growth and development, they create a safe space to reflect upon their limitations and challenges that hold them back from living their purpose. Having a partner to help you navigate these challenges and identify your purpose is what this seven-week journey is all about.

Miracles transpire when two people set foot on a journey, as collective energy and synergy generate creativity that benefits the people involved and everyone around them. As I travel across this country and outside its borders, I am constantly inspired and encouraged by the immense potential within the depths of each person I meet. From bustling cities to serene rural areas, I witness people from all walks of life striving to pursue their purpose. What holds them back from achieving their goal? A partnership

Section One
Part III:

A Partnership Approach

A partnership approach requires partners to be open to new ideas and perspectives during this seven-week process. Therefore, set aside preconceived notions, skepticism, doubt, or worry. These thought patterns create emotions that hinder and block what you come together to build. Next, each partner should actively engage with the material by taking notes, highlighting key passages, or journaling their thoughts weekly. Each weekend provides an opportunity to reflect on what you learned about yourself and your partner the previous week. This process helps your partnership engage in meaningful conversations about weekly insightfulness and reflect on your behavior, which allows for deeper self-analysis, meditation, and journaling. Always remind yourself that discovering one's purpose is a gradual process, and it is essential to take your time and effort when and if clarity does not come immediately. Implementing the suggested weekly exercises into your daily life will help you identify areas holding you back from embodying your purpose.

Below are three key steps to enhance your experience and ensure effective results. The steps below will equip you with the tools to embark on a transformative journey of self-discovery to live your purpose.

Step 1: Setting Clear Intentions

Please write down your intentions each week and review them with your partner before the week begins. This practice will help solidify your weekly commitment and keep you accountable. Another effective way to set clear intentions is by practicing *visualization*. Creating a mental blueprint can guide your actions by vividly imagining your desired outcomes. However, writing them down is the best way to remember who you promised to be during the week.

Trust The Process

Below, write down your intentions for this journey.

_____

_____

_____

Step 2: Embrace Honesty, Patience, and Taking Action

There are no "special" favors along this path. Therefore, what appears as a barrier should be addressed head-on and discussed to practice identifying these barriers in the future. The journey requires nothing but honesty, patience, and practicing taking action. Understand that self-discovery is a continual process, and it may take time to uncover your hidden fears, doubts, and worries that get in the way of your discovery. So, embrace setbacks as learning experiences and remain dedicated to exploring the untapped possibilities in the setbacks. Especially during challenging moments, ask yourself, "What am I pretending NOT to know about purpose? Your answer may surprise you.

Answer these three questions:

1. What am I pretending NOT to know about my purpose?

   _____

   _____

   _____

2. What excuses will I give to quit this process or make it complicated? Why?

   _____

   _____

   _____

   _____

   _____

   _____

3. List _three excuses you might give your partner when you want to quit - when things get complicated or challenging._

   _First Excuse:_____

   Second Excuse: _____

   Third Excuse: _____

Trust The Process

Step 3: Challenge Your Excuses –

Excuses often act as barriers, preventing us from taking risks and embracing our powerful talents and gifts. Excuses provide a false sense of security and allow us to justify our inaction or lack of progress. By challenging these excuses, we can dismantle the limitations they impose on us. It means questioning the validity of your excuses along this journey.

Step 3a: Identify "Where" Your Excuses Come From

Excuses come from a variety of sources, both internal and external. On an inner level, fear of failure or fear of success can give rise to excuses. When faced with the possibility of not achieving our goals or purpose, it is easier to make excuses than confront our fears head-on. Excuses can also result from external factors such as societal expectations or pressure from others. The fear of judgment or disappointment of those around us can lead to the creation of excuses as a protective mechanism. Excuses arise from a complex interplay of our internal struggles and external influences, highlighting the need for self-reflection and introspection to overcome them.

By implementing these three steps, you can break free from the cycle of making excuses and make significant strides toward living a purposeful life.

"Excuses are monuments of nothingness and they build bridges to nowhere."

By Author Carolyn McCall

Section One
Part IV:

The Journey is Filled With -
Mountains And Valleys

Celebrating the valleys is as vital as reaching the mountaintops. Success is not a smooth, straightforward, or linear path but a series of ups and downs. Mountains also symbolize the journey of self-discovery and personal growth. When we venture into the mountains, we are pushed out of our comfort zones, testing our limits and pushing ourselves to new heights. In this way, mountains become a metaphor for discovering our

purpose. They remind us that our growth for our purpose lies - *in the journey itself*, in the continuous climb toward self-improvement and fulfillment. Mountains teach us that it is through facing difficulties head-on that we can truly understand who we are and what we are capable of achieving.

On the other hand, in the context of discovering your purpose, the term "valley" can hold significant meaning, too. Symbolically, valleys often represent periods of challenge, struggle, or adversity in life. They are the low points, the moments of uncertainty and doubt. However, we can expand and learn the most about ourselves in these valleys. The valley signifies a pivotal moment of self-discovery and transformation. We can uncover our true selves, emerging stronger, wiser, and more resilient in these depths.

Therefore, take advantage of the valleys by facing your pain head-on during this journey - in doing so, you can open yourself up to deeper reflection.

"The valleys symbolize insightful perspectives and lessons learned.
The mountains represent great heights of achievement, awareness, freedom, and healing."

Section One
Part V:

How to Confront Fears –
Along This Journey

Confronting your fears - is the ONLY way you will live your purpose. People who face their fears believe in their power to overcome them. Practicing confronting fear is essential to learning, unlearning, and relearning how to face our fears and walk through them with courage, dignity, and confidence. Deliberately facing our fears is the place to start. Fear is a powerful emotion that can trigger our *fight-flight-freeze responses, which are* crucial in helping us respond to fearful situations or circumstances. For example, suppose a speeding car is driving the wrong way or weaving in and out of traffic on a busy highway. When faced with fear such as this, our bodies instinctively prepare for action. ***The fight response enables us to confront the threat head-on, summoning*** our courage and determination to move out of the way of danger.

However, **the flight response prompts us to escape** or avoid the source of fear altogether, ensuring our safety and preservation. ***<u>Lastly, the freeze response causes us to become momentarily paralyzed</u>,*** allowing us to assess the situation and decide how best to proceed. In this way, fear catalyzes our survival instincts, enabling us to navigate challenging circumstances and protect ourselves when necessary. The same emotional triggers are released with "false fear." False fear refers to the irrational and unfounded fears that hinder our ability to live our purpose. It is a psychological phenomenon often stems from past experiences or societal conditioning. False fear operates by *distorting* our perception of reality, making us believe that certain risks or challenges are far more threatening than they are. This distorted perception can paralyze us and prevent us from pursuing our dreams and desires. False fear triggers anxiety, doubt, and self-doubt, leading us to doubt our abilities and question the validity of our ambitions. Here's another example of "false fear:" When a child is told by a person of authority or someone they admire that they are not intelligent enough to go to college, what do they do? They do not pursue the opportunity to go to college and get a job at a local burger joint. They stay at the burger joint, never pursuing their purpose or having enough income to purchase a home or a new car. When we allow ourselves to be consumed by "false fear," it distorts our beliefs and prevents us from taking the necessary steps toward our hopes and dreams. These distorted beliefs often manifest as self-doubt, lack of confidence, and a fear of failure. As a result, we may find ourselves stuck in a cycle of complacency, settling for a life that does not align with our true passions and aspirations. When overcoming this, it is crucial to change our distorted beliefs.

Section One
Part VI:

False Fear vs. Perceived Fear

False fear and perceived fear may seem similar, but they have distinct differences. False fear refers to an irrational or unfounded sense of danger or threat. It is often rooted in imagination or past experiences blown out of proportion. On the other hand, *"Perceived Fear" is a genuine response to a real or potential threat.* Perceived fear can help us make informed decisions and take necessary precautions. Understanding the difference between false fear and perceived fear is crucial as it allows us to differentiate between baseless anxieties and genuine concerns that require our attention and action. Here is an example of false fear that can be seen in fear of failure. Many individuals fear taking risks or pursuing their passions because they fear failing. However, this fear is often unfounded, as failure is a natural part of learning. *On the other hand, perceived fear refers to fears based on assumptions or irrational beliefs.* For example, someone may fear public speaking because they believe they will embarrass themselves or be judged by others. These fears are often exaggerated and do not reflect the true outcome of the situation.

Dr. Martin Luther King Jr.'s Death –

Highlights the Coexistence of False and Perceived Fear

When Dr. King was assassinated, it is understandable that one might have experienced a sense of false fear, which arises from irrational thoughts or beliefs. However, it is also essential to acknowledge that perceived fear was present due to the genuine threat that existed on that day. The story below demonstrates how both fears can intertwine, emphasizing fear's complexity and subjective nature. April 4th, 1968, the day Dr. Martin Luther King Jr. died, profoundly impacted me at the tender age of six, leaving me traumatized and overwhelmed with fear. Experiencing the loss of such a prominent figure in my household devastated our entire family. The date and time are etched in my memory due to the trauma of that day. Everyone in my family was glued to the television, and we watched every detail of his assassination. During the broadcast, the announcer said, "Dr. Martin Luther King Jr. was dead." At that moment, my mom let out a yell I had never heard before, prompting me to run upstairs and hide under my bed. I thought the world was ending, so I stayed there all night, relying on the two corners of the wall to provide safety so the outside world could not hurt me. That night became a night that defined the rest of my life. Perceived fear shook my belief system to its core. Before that night, I believed the world was a safe place to live. After that night, the opposite was true, and I locked on to a belief that the world was not a safe place.

Trust The Process

All night, my mother described and talked about Dr. King's contributions to the world. She said he fought tirelessly for justice and equality for everyone, not just black people. Her words shook my young understanding of what justice and equality were. Suddenly, I became acutely aware through the newscast and the discussion within my family. Dr. King dedicated his life to fighting for civil rights and racial equality for everyone, not just me. To my mother, justice meant the fair and impartial treatment of all individuals, regardless of race or background. She believed everyone should have equal access to opportunities, resources, and rights without discrimination or prejudice. She always wanted to live in a society where everyone was judged based on the content of their character rather than the color of their skin.

My mother advocated for eradicating racial segregation and discrimination, emphasizing the importance of unity and brother and sisterhood among all people. His death became a traumatic event in our household— marking a turning point in my life as fear began to infiltrate my thoughts and actions. The fear that engulfed me stemmed from the realization that standing up for what I believed in could come at a significant cost. It was the day *"Perceived Fear"* ignited a journey within me. From that moment on, every morning when I wake up. I thought, "What traumatic event will happen today that I cannot prepare for?" My next thought was, "The world is terrifying, and I will hide from it as much as possible." The complexities of one's life experiences can be overwhelming, causing individuals to retreat into their shells and avoid facing the challenges of living authentically. Marianne Williamson's poem *"Our Deepest Fear"* reminds us that it is not our darkness but our authentic light that can intimidate ourselves and others.

Her poem is a powerful reminder that we must confront and overcome the insecurities and self-doubt that hold us back from living authentically. By embracing our unique gifts, we can confidently step into our purpose and make a meaningful impact on the world around us. Williamson encourages us to tap into the spiritual greatness in all of us. She encourages us to focus on our inner "light, "where our talent, inner genius, and magnificent power live. Our "light" is the lighthouse that permits others to shine their light. Fear drives us away from our light, which diminishes our view of what is possible for us. Therefore, along this journey, *shine your light and allow your partner to shine their light.* Spirituality is a deeply personal and subjective experience; what lights me spiritually may differ from others. Enlightenment comes from within; embracing that part of you is the key.

Section One
Part VII:

Setting YOUR Past Free – Requires Faith

Setting our *past free – requires Faith*. Our past experiences, especially the negative ones, often create a sense of fear and apprehension within us. These negative thought patterns keep us from progressing and hinder our personal growth. Acknowledging poor choices or painful life experiences can help us see that what happened in our past was necessary *for our* personal development. This way, our history no longer holds us captive. Past pain is a teacher, highlighting areas of our lives that require attention and improvement. It forces us to have Faith that these experiences came to teach us lessons we must learn to move forward. When we surrender our past pain and focus on the desires of our hearts, we allow God to work within us and transform our fears into Faith.

By replacing fear with Faith, we step out of fear and into Faith. The three steps below work harmoniously to help you learn, unlearn, and relearn how to have Faith. Remember Hebrews 11:1 in the King James Version; *"Now Faith is the substance hoped for, the evidence of things not seen."* Along this journey, practice Faith by practicing these three things:

- *First, Faith starts with Trusting GOD.* It will involve acknowledging that He has a more significant plan for your gifts and talents far exceeding yours. By surrendering your desires, God takes control and guides you toward His purpose.

- *Secondly, pray every day - along this journey.* Prayer keeps the line of communication open with God, which is crucial for your success. Regular conversations with God strengthen our relationship and allow us to seek His guidance. It aligns our desires with His will.

- *Third, demonstrate your commitment to your partner and your purpose through Faith.* It requires a willingness to follow the *light* that lights your path, even when it may be difficult or contrary to your desires, by trusting, praying, and being committed to this journey. You are exhibiting Faith.

Psalm 33:10-11 clarifies that the Lord sovereignly orchestrates our lives' details—
even our plans change. KJV

Trust The Process

Section One
Part VIII:

Practice Using Emotional Intelligence

What is Emotional Intelligence?

Emotional intelligence is the ability to understand, manage, and express emotions effectively within oneself and with others. Emotional intelligence is a foundation for cultivating empathy, fostering effective communication, and constructively resolving conflicts within a partnership. It encompasses a range of people skills, such as self-awareness, empathy, emotional regulation, and social skills. As we grow our Faith in God, emotional intelligence enables us to navigate our emotions and understand them in a God-centered way. By being self-aware, we can recognize when our thought patterns do not match up with the intentions of our hearts. This awareness helps us seek resolution peacefully rather than yield to our negative thought patterns. Emotional intelligence cultivates humility and selflessness, allowing us to surrender to God's divine plan.

How Do Emotional Intelligent Skills Benefit a Partnership?

Emotional intelligence skills play a crucial role in benefiting the partnership of discovering one's purpose. First, these skills enable individuals to understand better and manage their emotions, which is essential in self-discovery. By being aware of their feelings and how they impact their thoughts and actions, individuals can make more informed decisions about their purpose and align it with their true desires and values. Additionally, emotional intelligence skills foster empathy and understanding towards others, allowing individuals to build meaningful connections and collaborate effectively. This partnership thrives on open communication, trust, and support, all of which are enhanced by emotional intelligence skills.

Furthermore, emotional intelligence helps individuals navigate challenges and setbacks that may arise while pursuing one's purpose. Overall, emotional intelligence skills are valuable tools for promoting self-awareness, fostering connections with others, and enabling individuals to overcome obstacles.

Proverbs 23:7 KJB, "As a man thinketh in his heart, so is he."

Trust The Process

Five Components of Emotional Intelligence in a Partnership:

1. **Self-awareness:** Understanding one's emotions, needs, desires, and triggers is fundamental to emotional intelligence. This self-awareness allows individuals to communicate honestly and authentically with their partners, promoting openness and vulnerability in the relationship.

2. **Empathy:** Empathy, the ability to understand and share another person's emotions, is vital in establishing emotional intimacy. Partners who demonstrate empathetic behavior create a safe and supportive space, validating each other's feelings and experiences.

3. **Emotional Regulation:** Emotional regulation entails effectively managing emotions and responding to situations with emotional balance. Individuals with high emotional control can navigate conflicts and disagreements without resorting to harmful behaviors, fostering healthier and more constructive outcomes in their partnerships.

4. **Social Skills:** Social skills are integral to nurturing a harmonious partnership. These skills encompass effective communication, active listening, compromise, and cooperation. Partners with well-developed social skills are more likely to communicate their needs, resolve conflicts amicably, and maintain a solid emotional connection.

5. **Relationship Management:** Relationship management is an integral component of a partnership, as it plays a crucial role in fostering understanding, empathy, and effective communication between partners. This aspect of relationship management involves being aware of one's emotions and those of others and using this awareness to guide behavior and interactions. By practicing relationship management skills such as active listening, assertiveness, and conflict resolution, individuals can establish a harmonious partnership that promotes personal growth and fulfillment.

Trust The Process

Section One
Part IX:

Applying Emotional Intelligence Skills in Partnership

Emotional intelligence skills allow partners to recognize that trying new things creates insight, even though it feels overwhelming and pushes us outside our comfort zone. It can also help you manage your touchy-feely emotions and peel back the layers of your life to identify the emotional barriers that keep you stuck. When we understand that emotions are the energy behind our behavior, and if we do not acknowledge and manage them. They can stop a partnership's progress. Identifying these emotional thought patterns is the key to overcoming them. Hence, receiving feedback from your partner is essential. Your partner's feedback will help you unblock barriers and provide enormous insight into the opposite perspective. Therefore, please pay attention to what your partner says and does because you are succeeding when they are succeeding. When they fail, you fail in some area of your life. Why? Because you are your partner. You are a mirror to them, and they are a mirror of you. What you do, they do in some form or another.

Thus, it is crucial to prioritize enhanced communication, conflict resolution, emotional intimacy, and relationship connection skills. Investing in these four areas of emotional intelligence will significantly improve your relationship along this journey.

1. Enhanced Communication: Emotional intelligence promotes active listening, constructive feedback, and non-verbal cues, fostering effective partner communication. It leads to better mutual understanding and connection, reducing the likelihood of misunderstandings and resentment.

2. Conflict Resolution: With emotional intelligence, partners can approach conflicts with empathy and reason, seeking win-win solutions rather than resorting to aggression or avoidance. It ensures that conflicts become growth opportunities and strengthen the relationship bond.

3. Increased Emotional Intimacy: Emotional intelligence fosters a deep connection between partners by fostering vulnerability, trust, and understanding. This intimacy serves as the bedrock for discovering their purpose.

4. Relationship Connection: Partnerships with emotional intelligence tend to experience higher relationship connections. Emotionally intelligent individuals are more capable of meeting their partners' emotional needs, resulting in greater overall relationship fulfillment. Self-awareness is the most essential tool along this journey.

Affirmation:
"I am at the right place, at the right time. Thus, I am open to __all__ God has for me!"

Trust The Process

Section One
Part X:

Emotional Intelligence Affirmations

Emotional Intelligence affirmations aim to **state a truth** of expectancy and practice affirming it throughout the day. Exceptional and remarkable people know that affirming the right thoughts changes their outcomes. Reciting emotionally intelligent affirmations throughout the day is essential to living an extraordinary life. Daily affirmations are the catalyst for eliminating shame, doubt, worry, and guilt. It transforms the darkness into light. Elevating our spirit to focus on the light in the morning and throughout the day is *Giving Yourself Permission to be Phenomenal* daily.

Ten "Emotional Intelligence" Affirmations to practice along this journey:

1. I live in a joyous, expansive world that offers me the best life has to offer.
2. God is the source of my supply.
3. God's financial *prosperity* flows to me in an avalanche of abundance.
4. *Every day, I look to the living spiritual God within for Divine guidance.*
5. I accept *goodness* into my life, filling me with joy, love, and health.
6. God's riches flow to me easily every day.
7. New doors open for me because I am *worthy* of stepping through them with gratitude.
8. My feet support me to walk into my purpose, and my knees bend to keep me in prayer while my heart brings my intentions to fruition with the love and support of God.
9. Financial success supports me in all my endeavors.
10. Healthy food choices support my health and wellness, strengthening my body daily.
11. Reciting these affirmations every day will spark progress. Things move forward based on what we say to ourselves daily.

Affirm:
"I am happy, and my happiness elevates the heart of God!"

Section Two:

The seven pillars are necessary to pursue personal growth and development. Also, know that the exercises along this journey will push you and your partner outside your comfort zone, where growth, resilience, and self-discovery live. Therefore, rather than judging the activities and the process, it is essential to approach them with an open mind and embrace the opportunity and the new adventure that awaits you.

1. **Expanding Comfort Zones**: By engaging in activities outside your comfort zones, we open ourselves up to new awareness for growth. As we navigate unfamiliar territory, we gain valuable insights and improve our capabilities.

2. **Encouraging Creativity and Problem-Solving**: When confronted with challenges, think critically. It will foster creativity and enhance our problem-solving abilities. Remember, the exercises will push you to explore innovative approaches to overcome difficulties.

3. **Building Self-Confidence**: Increasing self-confidence requires you to accept and confront beliefs that hold you back from being your best self. These profoundly ingrained beliefs often limit our potential and hinder our personal growth.

4. **Acknowledging Subjective Perspectives**: It is essential to recognize that personal biases, beliefs, and experiences emotionally influence judgments. So, avoid judgment to create an environment conducive to personal growth.

5. **Utilizing Challenging Exercises Effectively**: Instead of shying away from discomfort or pain, we ask you to address it and acknowledge the opportunity and growth it provides. Owning our discomfort makes us more adept at navigating challenging situations.

6. **Seek Guidance And Support From Your Partner**: We must recognize that we don't have to face challenges alone. Seeking your partner's guidance is why a partnership along this journey is required. Partnerships provide valuable insights, encouragement, and practical advice.

7. **Reflect and Introspect**: After engaging in challenging exercises, reflect on the experiences weekly. Self-reflection allows for deeper understanding, helping us identify areas for improvement while recognizing our growth and achievements.

Trust The Process

Section Two:

How the Seven-Week Process Works

Several key elements are required to embark on a journey of self-discovery alongside another person. The most essential requirement is simple - have an open mind to embrace new challenges that you identify your purpose. Remember that the awareness of your need to change is part of the journey, and it may arrive uninvited, unsought after, and suddenly. You are right where you need to be to experience a breakthrough. Your job is not to ignore, resist, or fear the moment. But use it as a catalyst for personal awareness and self-discovery. Push through the discomfort by forcing yourself to confront the pain. Embracing pain as a means of growth is the gateway to the change you seek. It could uncover what is in the way of acknowledging or knowing your purpose.

Also, a keen sense of curiosity is essential. Asking questions, seeking knowledge, and delving into different experiences will help you better understand yourself and your passions. Furthermore, patience is vital on this journey. Discovering one's purpose takes time and self-reflection, so be patient with your partner and yourself. It will help you both tremendously. Lastly, a genuine willingness to be vulnerable and reflective is the ingredient that will transform your life.

Along this journey, know that transformative experiences will unfold. Be careful when this happens. Seeking support and guidance from loved ones is essential; being mindful of their potential influence is crucial because they may not understand your journey. However, once you have shared your goals and desires for this journey, in most cases, your family and friends will support you. But, if their response is filled with skepticism, doubt, or even discouragement, you must limit what you share with them. It is advisable to choose whom you confide in. Choosing to confide in your partner is why you have a partner - they can provide the necessary encouragement and understanding without undermining your progress.

Seven Weeks to Your Purpose

During this 7-week journey of self-discovery, you can expect to embark on a transformative experience that will enable you to live your life with purpose and intention. Throughout the journey, you will delve deep into your inner self, exploring your passions, values, and desires. Alongside this self-exploration, you will also receive guidance on setting meaningful goals and creating an action plan to align your life with your purpose with a partnership's support, love, and power. By the end of this journey, you and your partner can expect to have a renewed sense of direction, a stronger connection to your authentic self, and the tools necessary to live a purpose-driven life.

Week 1: Find A Partner

Inviting someone into our personal space requires careful consideration, as it involves opening our minds and hearts to another individual. Self-discovery and understanding one's purpose can be complex and challenging; having a supportive partner by your side can make a significant difference. However, choosing a partner who respects your journey and offers genuine support is essential, as their influence can impact your growth and development. Therefore, finding a partner who aligns with your values, shares similar goals, and exhibits a genuine interest in your personal growth is essential in this mental choice of inviting someone into our space.

Week 2: Get To Know Your Partner

The second week focuses on getting to know your partner, which is vital to achieving your goal along this journey. Your journey of self-discovery is *not meant to be solitary*; it is through our connections with others that we utterly understand and discover ourselves. Your partner can serve as a mirror, reflecting your strengths and weaknesses and helping us uncover hidden talents and passions we may have overlooked or taken for granted. When we share our dreams and aspirations with partners, we invite them into our hearts and souls. It is where our most authentic selves reside, our deepest emotions are felt, and our most cherished memories are kept in this space. Therefore, this place should be honored and valued, for it holds the essence of who you are. This act of sharing is an intimate gesture that requires trust, understanding, and mutual respect.

Trust The Process

Week 3: Discovering The Influence of Upbringing on Your Purpose

As we progress through this journey, peeling back the layers of our family dynamics is crucial. Families are intricate systems with unique personalities, histories, and relationships. These dynamics can both shape and challenge our pursuit to live our purpose. Family roles and responsibilities can sometimes limit one's ability to explore one's purpose. We can gain valuable insights by untangling the influences that have shaped our beliefs, values, and perspectives.

Week 4: Listening to God's Quiet Answers "Our Anchor"

Listening to God's whispers transcends our limited perspective and uncovers the hidden answers we've been seeking. These whispers carry a depth of wisdom that surpasses our understanding. They provide us with guidance and direction that cannot be found through our efforts alone. In these moments, we uncover the profound truths that have eluded us, giving us an anchor to hold onto during life's storms.

Week 5: Self-Love "Wholeness"

The journey of week six involves embracing your light through the power of self-love. When we practice self-love, we admit our flaws and allow our authentic selves to emerge. Wholeness can come in many ways; one perspective is that it comes from God. Connecting with your spirituality can bring a profound sense of purpose and fulfillment. Believing a higher power is guiding you and directing your path instills a sense of hope and trust as you discover your purpose. It is the power of week six.

Week 6: No More Victim Story – Change is Here

The goal of week five is to accept blame for our circumstances or external factors. Those with victim stories often share their story with anyone who listens. This mindset limits our ability to learn from the lesson and heal. This week's learning, unlearning, and relearning involves identifying and acknowledging your role in creating the situation or circumstances. This acknowledgment sparks the growth you need from the experience.

Week 7: The Potter's Wheel

Just as a potter skillfully uses the wheel to transform a lump of clay into a beautiful vessel, God, too, works in our lives to mold us into vessels of His purpose. Through the whispers of His presence, God offers us answers and direction, gently guiding us toward our true calling. On this wheel of life, we experience growth and transformation and ultimately discover our purpose when we surrender ourselves to the steady hands of the Divine Potter.

Focus on Your "LIGHT"

This light represents our inner wisdom, intuition, and passion, illuminating our path. By focusing on your **"Light,"** you can navigate your challenges and setbacks along this journey with resilience and determination. It will also align with your calling. By embracing the **Light,** you allow yourself to tap into your full potential and experience a profound sense of fulfillment and purpose in every step of this transformative journey. Throughout this seven-week journey, "Let Your **"Light"** Shine!" My sister Debra has a sign in the bathroom that says, "This little light of mine, I'm gonna let it shine…." Most of us have heard this catchy tune. It comes from Matthew 5:16: *"Let your light shine before others, so that they may see your good works."* We can change our world when we stop ignoring the **"Light"** that wants to shine through each of us.

In 2018 India, Arie illuminated the stage at the 2018 Grammy Awards Premier Ceremony by singing a song she wrote in 2013 called "I Am Light." Her message in the song announces that we are all – light. We are not the things our family did - nor the voices in our heads. *We are light.* We are not the color of our eyes nor the skin on the outside. *WE ARE LIGHT!* We are all stars, a piece of it all. *We Are Light.* Please listen to this song before you start week one. I hope it helps you see yourself as the unique and rare jewel that you are. No one has your light; the courage to shine is what this journey is about. India Arie learned that Wayne Dyer listened to her song at Hana, in the mountains of Maui, in Hawaii. It touched him so much that he wrote his next book. This song inspired me to add this story before I published the book. I am happy that I did.

John 18:2
Jesus said, "I am the Light of the World."

The Three Levels of (Self)

"Breath of Body, Psyche, and Spirit"

The three levels of (self) have fascinated scholars, philosophers, and thinkers across various disciplines throughout history. Understanding the (self) is a complex endeavor comprising multiple dimensions that intertwine and interact with one another. This journey will delve into the three levels of the self: the breath of the body, the psyche or mind, and the spirit. By exploring each level, we aim to comprehensively understand the intricate nature of human nature to help you along this journey.

The First Level

THE BREATH OF BODY: "EMI"

In the Yoruba language, the concept of the *breath of the body* is referred to as **"Emi."** This term encompasses more than just the physical act of breathing; it delves into a more profound understanding of life force and vitality. In Yoruba culture, **"Emi"** is believed to be the essence that animates our physical being and connects us to the divine. It is considered a sacred and powerful energy that sustains our existence and influences our well-being. Our breath is the vital energy that sustains our existence and connects us to the world. This level of self, rooted in the tangible and material aspects of our being, serves as level one in this journey. The Yoruba people recognize the profound importance of this breath in maintaining a healthy and balanced life, highlighting its integral role in their cultural understanding of self.

Taking care of ourselves on this journey involves paying attention to our diet and overall health. Thus, eating healthy, nutrient-rich foods fuels our bodies to function optimally. So, exercising weekly and practicing self-care routines such as getting enough sleep and staying hydrated contributes to maintaining a vibrant body. By prioritizing these aspects of self-care, we can ensure that our physical well-being remains strong along this journey.

The Second Level

THE PSYCHE: "The Power to Change"

In the Yoruba language, the concept of psyche represents the "**Power to Change.**" The statement

that the psyche is the most flexible to change through *neuroplasticity* holds significant truth. Neuroplasticity refers to the brain's ability to reorganize and form new neural connections throughout life. Unlike the breath of the body, which is primarily influenced by physiological factors, and the spirit, which embodies our core values and beliefs, the psyche is more pliable and adaptable.

Through neuroplasticity, our brains can rewire neural pathways associated with our thoughts and emotions, leading to changes in behavior and perception. This flexibility allows individuals to learn new skills, overcome traumatic experiences, and develop healthier thought patterns. It can be concluded that the psyche is the most willing to make change. So, care enough to confront and challenge profound ingrained thought patterns that no longer serve you along this journey.

However, know that changing your mind is not a quick fix but a gradual process that requires patience and affirming yourself daily. Affirmations are powerful tools to counteract negative thoughts and beliefs that hinder our personal growth. This rewiring replaces self-doubt with self-confidence. We cultivate a healthier attitude and perspective when we engage in positive self-talk and acknowledge our worth and abilities.

The psyche represents the vast realm of thoughts, emotions, memories, and conscious awareness that characterizes our subjective experience. Our beliefs, values, and perceptions shape the psyche, influencing our understanding of self and others. Our intellect is where we grapple with our dreams, fears, doubts, and aspirations. Our thoughts create intricate webs of meaning, shaping our identities and influencing our choices. The psyche is the wellspring of creativity, imagination, and introspection, allowing us to explore the depths of our inner world and make changes. It harnesses and initiates the power of change.

Trust The Process

The Third Level

The Spirit: "My Light"

In the Yoruba language, **"My Light"** holds great significance as it represents the spirit at the highest level of self. In this context, the spirit is seen as a luminous essence that illuminates and guides one's journey through life. This "Light," which resides within us, connects us to our higher power and is a

source of divine wisdom and intuition. Our **"Light"** represents God, an intangible essence within us that seeks connection and meaning beyond our existence. Within the soul realm, we encounter the concepts of one's purpose, where wholeness and universal interconnectedness live.

The spirit encompasses our quest for spirituality and our search for something greater than ourselves. This level of self-confidence invites us to explore questions about the nature of our existence, the meaning of life, and our place in the grand tapestry of existence. Through the spirit, we find solace, inspiration, and a sense of belonging to something more significant than the self. The labyrinth concept extends to the spirit realm, signifying a deeper connection with our higher selves and the divine. In essence, the labyrinth serves as a powerful metaphor for exploring and understanding the complexities of our existence on all three levels of self.

In pursuing personal growth and self-improvement, it is often tempting to engage in self-criticism and attack ourselves for our perceived flaws and shortcomings. However, a more constructive approach lies in understanding and embracing the three levels of self - the breath of body, psyche, and spirit. Rather than attacking ourselves, we should strive to change ourselves. This shift in perspective encourages us to focus on self-awareness, self-acceptance, and self-transformation. By recognizing the interconnectedness of these three levels, we can cultivate a holistic approach to personal development that nurtures our physical well-being, emotional resilience, and spiritual growth. Through change, we can develop a sense of gratitude for Everything we have been through, which propels us toward personal growth and fulfillment.

The "Psyche" Level Two:

Distorted Words, Thoughts, And Behaviors

Level Two is the psyche, and it is the function that encompasses the entirety of our mental and emotional states. It is a complex system that governs our thoughts, feelings, and behaviors. However, when it comes to negative words, they often serve as a reflection of how we perceive ourselves. The psyche plays a crucial role in shaping our self-image and self-esteem. Negative remarks can easily seep into our consciousness and become internalized, leading to a negative perception of ourselves. They can reinforce insecurities and contribute to mental health issues such as anxiety and depression. Therefore, it is essential to recognize negative words, thoughts, and behaviors and how they impact our psyche. Your job is to foster a positive self-image through self-awareness, self-compassion, and self-leadership with affirming words, thoughts, and behaviors throughout this seven-week process.

Listed below are three ways to recognize distorted words, thoughts, and behavior:

I. Know That Self-Talk is Automatic (Habitual):

Your self-talk is automatic, habitual, and fueled by prejudices against oneself or others. They can emerge in various forms, such as overgeneralization, exaggeration of negatives, personalization, and many more. These distorted thoughts often contribute to unnecessary anxiety, depression, low self-esteem, and other emotional disturbances.

II. Practice Being Self-Aware

Self-awareness is the flashlight that illuminates our minds' words, thoughts, and behaviors, allowing us to discern distorted words, thoughts, and behaviors from accurate ones. When people understand the underlying mental processes, they can step back and think about the thoughts that created their words, thoughts, and behaviors. Through this awareness, people develop a cognitive understanding of how change happens.

III. Mindfulness-Journaling-Receiving Feedback:

1. Mindfulness Meditation: This practice is renowned for enhancing self-awareness.

2. Journaling: Journaling is a powerful tool for self-awareness. By writing down thoughts and emotions, individuals can objectively assess their experiences.

3. Receiving Feedback: Actively seeking and receiving feedback from your trusted partner — can further enhance your self-awareness of negative habitual thought patterns.

IV. Strategies for Challenging Distorted Words, Thoughts, and Behaviors: The next step is to challenge these words, thoughts, and behaviors by replacing them with constructive ones.

Practice These Three Methods:

1. Cognitive (Mental) Restructuring: This technique examines the evidence supporting and refuting distorted words, thoughts, and behaviors. *Questioning the validity of these words, thoughts, and behaviors* breaks the cycle of distorted thinking and behaviors. Weekly affirmations in the form of *"Permission Slips"* will be provided, along with emotional intelligence affirmations, which can be used to start this process. Please create your own as well.

Samples: Distorted Words, Thoughts, and Behaviors

1. I'm not smart enough.
2. I'm not pretty enough.
3. These things always happen to me.
4. I can't do that because of gender, color, or race.
5. I overeat when I am depressed or sad.
6. Nobody likes me. I hate myself
7. I could never see myself successful because…
8. I have sex and take drugs when upset or happy.
9. I feel useless and insecure; therefore, I can't move forward.
10. I go from relationship to relationship without learning the lessons from the previous relationship.

Which three distorted sentences above do you need to STOP saying, thinking, and doing?

1. _____

2. _____

3. _____

Trust The Process

Below, list one negative word, thought, and behavior you want to change along this journey.

Word (s): _____

Thought (s): _____

Behavior (s): _____

Below, list one word, thought, and behavior THAT confidently describes you.

The WORDS that represent confidence in me is…	The THOUGHT PATTERNS that represent confidence in me are…	The BEHAVIORS that represent confidence in me are…

2. Thought Records: Thought records are valuable tools that allow individuals to deconstruct their distorted thoughts. By recording the situation, emotions, and automatic thoughts associated with an event, individuals can objectively challenge and replace distorted thoughts with more rational and balanced ones.

3. Name the Emotion Out Loud: Learning to verbalize emotions can serve as a cathartic release, helping individuals process and manage their feelings more effectively. Naming emotions and reciting them aloud is essential to promote emotional awareness, communication skills, and overall well-being.

Mahatma Gandi said,

"Your beliefs become your thoughts. Your thoughts become your words. Your words become your actions. Your actions become your habits.

Carolyn's Distorted Words, Thoughts, & Behaviors

Dyslexia - Divine Order

I almost missed *my purpose* because of the distorted words, thoughts, and behaviors I created in my mind when I failed the third grade. The experience mortified me. Flunking the third grade was humiliating. At that moment, I felt and believed I was "dumb and stupid." These were my new thought patterns. Little did I know this was a purposeful life-altering experience that required me to take a journey inside myself to overcome this obstacle. Here's my story.

In 1970, I was eight and in the third grade. My third-grade teacher was Ms. Smith—one day when my twin sister Cheryl and I arrived at school. Our teacher (Ms. Smith) asked us to follow her down the hall to another classroom. When we arrived, the students were shouting and using profanity, and no teacher was in sight. At that moment, I was shocked and offended by my third-grade teacher's message to us. In my eight-year-old mind, she said, *"You and your twin sister are no longer smart enough to be in my classroom!"* Of course, that is not what she said, but it might have been in my head. I was devastated inside! I already felt insecure and stupid because of my grades and quiet personality. At that moment, the words, thoughts, and behavior changed instantly. I was no longer the same. Yes, I was angry, embarrassed, and ashamed, but also inspired, motivated, and determined! I did not know my cognitive mind could be an affirming place.

I began to affirm a new thought and belief about myself and what I could achieve. After that, every time I saw Ms. Smith. I confirmed my new thought pattern by saying to myself, *"I am going to college and prove YOU wrong about me."* Years later, I struggled to graduate from high school. But I graduated and went straight to college. I struggled in college and got kicked out of school. I begged my mother to help me get back in, and she did. She met with the Dean. After meeting with him, she suggested I get tested for dyslexia. Her foresight speaks highly of her love and compassion for me because the results returned positive. *Talk about Great News.* We both were elated. Why? Because the reason I flunked the third grade had a name, and it wasn't Ms. Smith. It was called dyslexia. It takes courage to *BE NEW*; in this moment, I was made *NEW!* My first thought was, "I'm NOT dumb and stupid after all." What was wrong with me had a name – dyslexia." I was grateful to my mother for suggesting I get tested. I am even more thankful for getting kicked out of school because this "perceived" negative experience was the catalyst that led to the discovery of my learning disability. The experience taught me that "perceived fear" can be what we need to make us new.

Trust The Process

Introduction to "Permission Slips"

One of the most significant barriers to living a purposeful life is due to fear, worry, and self-doubt. Permission slips provide a tool to confront and overcome these challenges. By granting yourself permission to make mistakes, take risks, and embrace uncertainty. Permission slips serve as a gateway, giving us a green light to explore new interests, acquire new skills, and aspire to be who we were born to be. People can navigate beyond their comfort zones and open themselves to endless possibilities by giving themselves permission. Permission is consent, which empowers us to break free from self-imposed limitations and take hold of the endless opportunities that await us on our journey toward self-discovery and personal development.

Hence, permission slips can profoundly impact our journey. When we acknowledge and confront our fears, learn to embrace imperfections, and nurture personal growth, we unlock our true potential and pave the way for a fulfilling, purpose-driven life. **By granting ourselves permission, we step out of the shadows and into the light**, embracing a life that aligns with our deepest aspirations. *Let us remember that permission slips are not mere pieces of paper or statements but a symbol of self-empowerment and liberation, enabling us to feel and be our most powerful selves.*

*Permission slips act as a **BEACON OF LIGHT**, illuminating the path toward our purpose and granting us the courage to ask for what we truly want. They encourage us to shed our inhibitions and embrace the possibilities that lie ahead, reminding us that we are worthy of living a life that aligns with our true calling.*

Ephesians 1:11 states, "Everything that transpires is woven into the purpose of God. Nothing that happens is outside of his will.

Trust The Process

Practice Reciting Your -

Permission Slips "3 Times A Day For 5 Minutes"

Giving ourselves permission to be phenomenal is an essential practice that can truly transform our lives

if we **practice checking in with ourselves three times a day for five minutes.** Incorporating this assignment into our daily lives allows us to practice standing guard over our words, thoughts, and behavior throughout the day. The process of checking in with our words, thoughts, and behaviors involves taking a step back from our everyday routines to observe and evaluate our thinking patterns consciously.

Replacing negative thoughts with positive ones requires a deliberate and sustained effort. Some effective strategies for fostering positive thinking include.

- Practice gratitude.
- Surround yourself with positive influences.
- Engage in self-care activities.

These practices provide a solid foundation for constructing a more optimistic mindset over time. In summary, checking in with our words, thoughts, and behavior is an essential process that helps us confront and replace negative thought patterns with more positive and empowering ones. You can shift and change your behavior and outcomes by developing self-awareness and employing cognitive restructuring techniques. Remember, embracing positivity is a journey that requires ongoing commitment, but the rewards are immeasurable.

Using *"permission slips"* throughout the day can significantly contribute to maintaining a positive mindset. *Permission slips* are powerful statements that help reframe negative thoughts and replace them with positive ones. By consciously repeating them, you can train your brain to focus on the positive aspects of your life. *Permission slips* remind us of our worth, capabilities, and potential, boosting our self-confidence. They serve as a mental reset button, redirecting your words, thoughts, and behaviors toward positivity and enabling us to navigate the day's challenges with optimism and a more positive outlook, which leads to increased motivation, productivity, and overall happiness.

THREE RULES for using "Permission Slips" daily.

This three-step process offers a practical approach to shifting our mindset and cultivating a positive outlook throughout the day.

- **First Rule:** Each morning, midday, and at the end of the day, begin to be aware of your negative words, thought patterns, and behaviors by writing them down in your journal. Acknowledging their presence during this process is crucial. It helps you gain the power, courage, and insight to challenge and change them. Writing them down builds your awareness, allowing you to change them daily.

- **Second Rule:** Challenge these negative thoughts by questioning their validity and replacing them with your positive "permission slip" affirmation for the week. Write your "permission slip" affirmation next to the negative words, thoughts, and behaviors you want to change. Pause and ask yourself, "Why do you allow these negative words, thoughts, and behaviors to exist in your life?" This step requires conscious effort and self-reflection, as we must identify the underlying beliefs fueling our negative thinking and behaviors.

- **Third Rule:** Practice reaffirming these positive thoughts throughout the day. You can rewire your brain by consistently reinforcing positive affirmations and teaching yourself to focus on more optimistic and empowering words, thoughts, and behaviors. This process is called neuroplasticity.

These three rules enhance the power of "permission slips" and pave the way for you to give yourself permission to be phenomenal! *See the list of weekly "permission slips" on the next page.*

Weekly "Permission Slip" Affirmations

Give yourself permission to affirm yourself daily. Repeating these affirmations throughout the week provides guidance and wisdom toward your goals. They serve as a powerful tool for self-reflection and growth, enabling you to stay connected to this insightful journey. **Recite three times a day for five minutes.**

Week 1: Permission Slip. "I have a supportive partner who is honest and trustworthy with me along this journey."
Week 2: Permission Slip. "I have a partner I can TRUST, and I'm a partner that is *TRUSTWORTHY!*"
Week 3: Permission Slip. "I grant myself permission to UNCOVER AND APPRECIATE how my parents or guardian prepared me for my purpose."
Week 4: Permission Slip. "God anchors me, and I listen to His quiet answers."
Week 5: Permission Slip. "I give myself permission to mend the broken pieces within me by opening the door to self-love, self-acceptance, and self-growth!" & "I am worthy of ALL great things God has for me."
Week 6: Permission Slip. "I grant myself permission to CHALLENGE MY VICTIM story by making it my PHENOMENAL story!" Romans 8:28 says, "All things work together for good to those who love God and are called according to His purpose."
Week 7: Permission Slip. "I give myself permission to *DISCOVER MY PURPOSE!*"

Trust The Process

Week One

FIND A PARTNER

Section Two
Week One:
Find A Partner

"The number one represents new beginnings."

The number one holds significant spiritual and euphoric meaning across various cultures and belief systems. Spiritually, the number one represents unity, wholeness, divine power, and new beginnings. It symbolizes the ultimate source of creation and the origin of all things. In many spiritual traditions, it is associated with the concept of oneness, reminding individuals of their interconnectedness with the Divine. Euphorically, number one signifies individuality, uniqueness, and self-confidence. It encourages individuals to embrace their authentic selves and stand tall in their identity. *Therefore, week one is truly an exciting new beginning!*

Week One Permission Slip:
"I have a supportive partner who is honest and trustworthy with me along this journey."
Recite three times a day for five minutes daily.

Hence, when finding a partner who will support you and has your back, recite the daily "permission slip" 3 times a day for five minutes. Reciting affirmations reinforces the idea that what we do is worthwhile and meaningful. We essentially affirm our actions and goals by repeating positive statements or beliefs. This practice can be beneficial during self-doubt or when faced with obstacles.

When encountering resistance, whether internal or external. Remember, resistance can be seen as a valuable indicator referencing the obstacles, challenges, and discomfort that arise when pursuing an endeavor that leads you to your purpose. The pushback and leaning forward into discomfort allow us to embark on a journey of self-discovery. In finding your partner, resistance should be interpreted as the right person is ready and willing to take this journey with you. This mindset shows that *you are pushing boundaries and exploring new territories.* It signifies that you are stepping outside your familiar realm and challenging yourself to grow. Resistance can manifest in various forms, such as self-doubt, fear of failure, or societal expectations. However, it is essential to recognize that resistance does not necessarily imply that the pursuit is futile. Instead, it should be viewed as an opportunity for reflection, growth, and resiliency. By embracing and overcoming resistance, we can uncover our true passions and align ourselves with a meaningful and fulfilling purpose.

Trust The Process

This week's goal is to find a partner. Your partner will provide you with

a unique opportunity to see yourself through the mirror of partnership. When you engage in collaborative effort through partnership, you expose yourself to different perspectives, ideas, and experiences that challenge your existing beliefs and assumptions. This exposure to diverse viewpoints allows you to reflect upon your thoughts and actions, enabling you to understand yourself better.

Therefore, a partnership is indeed *priceless,* as it has the potential to shape your life and influence your beliefs and behaviors in positive ways. Choosing the right partner can profoundly impact this journey and potentially last a lifetime. Partnership and purpose are intricately linked, as a supportive and compatible partner can provide the necessary encouragement and motivation to pursue one's goals and aspirations. In this sacred union, the number one represents the strength and stability of unity in a priceless partnership.

Partnership Characteristics- Integrity and Loyalty

INTEGRITY

Integrity is an essential quality that must be significantly valued in a partner and one that each partner should strive to embody within the partnership. When partners demonstrate integrity, they are honest, trustworthy, and emotionally available when you need them. An emotionally available partner is crucial in fostering a healthy and fulfilling relationship. Such a partner can connect emotionally with their significant other, allowing for open and honest communication. They are attentive and responsive to their partner's needs, providing support and understanding when necessary. An emotionally available partner is willing to be vulnerable, sharing their emotions and experiences without fear of judgment or rejection. They can express empathy and compassion, making their partner feel heard and valued. Overall, an emotionally available partner creates a safe and nurturing environment where individuals can grow and thrive together. Therefore, transparency and authenticity in your words and actions are required. You can build mutual respect and have honest communication by upholding these principles. Patience is another crucial characteristic of this partnership. It allows for understanding, empathy, and the willingness to work through difficulties together. It ensures that commitments are honored, and trust is upheld.

Trust The Process

LOYALTY

Loyalty is essential when in partnership. A loyal partner stands by your side through thick and thin, demonstrating unwavering support and commitment. They are trustworthy and reliable, always keeping their promises and remaining faithful to their word. In a partnership, loyalty fosters a sense of security and trust, which creates an opportunity for transparency. A loyal partner helps create a safe space where open communication and vulnerability can thrive, enabling the partners to navigate challenges with positive solutions, resilience, and unity. Ultimately, having a loyal partner not only strengthens the bond between partners but also enhances the overall purpose of the partnership – to grow, support, and empower one another unconditionally.

Identify three of the twelve characteristics listed above that you want in a partnership:

First characteristic: _____

Second characteristic: _____

Third characteristic: _____

Partnership Characteristics

1. Integrity	7. Loyalty
2. Self-Awareness	8. Reliable
3. Deep Listener	9. Accountable
4. Authentic	10. Communicate THOUGHTFULLY
5. Risk-Taker	11. Flexible
6. Patient	12. Honesty

The qualities I need and want most for this partnership to thrive and be successful are:

_____

_____

_____

The qualities I lacked consistency in the past - when in partnership are:

_____

_____

Partnership Confidentiality Agreement

Confidentiality serves as the foundation for this partnership. If confidentiality is broken the partnership is compromised. Trust, respect, integrity, and loyalty are destroyed when this happens.

PARTNERSHIP CONFIDENTIALITY AGREEMENT

PARTNERSHIP CONFIDENTIALITY IS AN ESSENTIAL ASPECT THAT MUST BE UPHELD THROUGHOUT THE JOURNEY OF THIS COLLABORATION. IT ENSURES THAT INFORMATION SHARED BETWEEN PARTNERS REMAINS SECURE AND PROTECTED, FOSTERING AN ENVIRONMENT OF TRUST AND MUTUAL RESPECT. CONFIDENTIALITY ALLOWS PARTNERS TO FREELY EXCHANGE IDEAS, STRATEGIES, AND SENSITIVE DATA WITHOUT THE FEAR OF IT BEING SHARED WITH EXISTING PARTNERSHIPS SUCH AS SPOUSES, KIDS, SIBLINGS, NEIGHBORS, CO-WORKERS, BOSSES, AND FRIENDS. THIS PARTNERSHIP IS SACRED! THEREFORE, PLEASE MAINTAIN CONFIDENTIALITY SO THAT YOUR PARTNER CAN FEEL CONFIDENT IN SHARING THEIR THOUGHTS AND CONCERNS OPENLY, KNOWING THAT THEIR INFORMATION WILL NOT BE DIVULGED OUTSIDE THE PARTNERSHIP. THIS COMMITMENT AND PRACTICE ULTIMATELY STRENGTHEN THE BOND BETWEEN PARTNERS AND ENABLES PARTNERS TO WORK TOGETHER TOWARD THEIR SHARED PURPOSE.

THROUGHOUT THIS JOURNEY, YOU BOTH ARE ESTABLISHING TRUST WITH ONE ANOTHER, WHICH IS WHY YOUR CONVERSATIONS MUST BE CONFIDENTIAL. THIS I S VITAL FOR THIS PROCESS TO BE SUCCESSFUL!

Please sign the "Partnership Confidentiality Agreement" below.

Your signature indicates that you agree and adhere to the confidentiality agreement above.

Partner (A) signed signature: _____ Date: _____

Partner (B) signed signature: _____ Date: _____

Partnership & Reciprocity

Reciprocity is a crucial element for a partnership to be balanced and effective. When both parties engage in reciprocal actions, it creates a sense of fairness and equality, fostering trust and cooperation. In any personal or professional partnership, the exchange of resources, efforts, and support should be mutual. Without reciprocity, there is a risk of one party feeling exploited or taken advantage of, leading to resentment and imbalance. By practicing reciprocity, individuals can ensure their contributions are acknowledged and valued, creating a harmonious and productive partnership. Therefore, reciprocity is necessary for a partnership to thrive.

In teaching people to walk in their purposeful path, a reciprocal partnership entails a collaborative and supportive alliance where the teacher and the learner contribute equally to each other's growth and development. It goes beyond a one-sided knowledge exchange and involves both parties' active engagement, respect, and empathy. In contrast, the learner and teacher actively participate, ask questions, and share their insights and experiences. The essence of a reciprocal partnership lies in its ability to foster a sense of empowerment, trust, and shared responsibility, ultimately enabling individuals to navigate their purposeful paths with confidence and fulfillment.

Several factors can hinder the establishment of a reciprocal partnership. Firstly, a lack of trust and communication can be a significant obstacle. Without open and honest communication, it becomes difficult to understand each other's needs and goals, leading to a breakdown in the partnership. Additionally, conflicting interests and priorities can impede the development of a reciprocal partnership. If both parties have different objectives or are focused on their gains rather than collective success, it becomes challenging to work together effectively. Moreover, power imbalances can create barriers to achieving a reciprocal partnership. When one party holds more authority or resources than the other, it can lead to unequal decision-making and limited collaboration.

Trust The Process

Reciprocity Exercise:

"Give Up the Need to..."

To create a reciprocal relationship, partners must relinquish the need to be right, first, and in control. These are self-sabotaging behaviors in a partnership. An example would be *withholding information*, being overly critical, defensive during discussions, harboring resentment, *avoiding conflict resolution*, or failing to take responsibility for one's actions. These behaviors hinder the partnership's progress and contribute to a harmful and unproductive journey. Partners must immediately recognize and address these self-sabotaging tendencies along this journey to foster healthy and purposeful alliances based on trust, transparency, and shared values.

When partners prioritize these aspects, they lay the groundwork for a robust, purposeful relationship that can withstand challenges to elevate and evolve into the perfectly undeniable, radiant evolution, which is what this journey is all about.

List three things *you must give up* to create a healthy reciprocal relationship with your partner.

1. I need to give up the need to _____
2. I need to give up the need to _____
3. I need to give up the need to _____

What will you do differently to change this behavior?

_____
_____
_____
_____
_____
_____
_____
_____

Share your answers with your partner when you get one in week two.

When You Might Have to End a Partnership

Several years ago, I coached and mentored someone. Unfortunately, at the time, I had no idea how profound their physical and psychological abuse was as a child and even as a young adult. I was stunned when she shared the graphic details of her abuse. At that moment, I could only say, "Thank you for sharing such delicate and private information with me." I ended the conversation immediately because I was uncomfortable discussing it further. My reaction to the information made her uncomfortable. Then, I hugged her and immediately asked if she had seen a licensed therapist. She said no. I then told her that because I was not a trained, licensed therapist, we needed to end the conversation and make an appointment for them to see one. They agreed. At that moment, I grabbed my cell phone and made an appointment. They were thrilled!

Today, they are thriving. Their story exemplifies the power of partnership along this journey. Recognizing your partner's need for professional help and taking the initiative to arrange therapy demonstrates a strong sense of collaboration and support. By actively helping your partner, you put them on the road to recovery and healing. You not only fulfilled your role as a caring partner but also played a pivotal role in helping your partner overcome an emotional trauma they need to heal. In order to move forward in their purpose. This powerful example highlights how partnership and purpose are intricately intertwined; supporting your partner can ultimately lead to a person's sense of purpose in life. Who knows what lies ahead for this individual and their journey? Everything happens for a reason and is ripe for you during a particular season.

Congratulations!

You have a partner!

Please write their name below.

My partner is _____.   Date: _____

Week Two

GETTING TO KNOW

YOUR PARTNER

Section Two
Week Two:

Getting to Know Your Partner

"The number two represents unity, balance, and partnership."

The number two symbolizes co-creating with God or with a partner to bring forth one's unique expression of unity into forms of new life. It represents opposites coming together, such as light and dark, male and female, or yin and yang. The concept of harmony and unity is often associated with the number two, as it signifies the need for balance in life. The number two can also signify partnerships and relationships, highlighting the importance of cooperation and collaboration. It embodies the idea that two individuals can come together to create a harmonious whole, where each person provides support, understanding, and stability to the other. The spiritual connotation of number two reminds us of the importance of cooperation, compromise, and mutual respect in fostering healthy relationships. Overall, it emphasizes that nothing is created by the self alone.

Week Two Permission Slip:

"I have a partner I can TRUST, and I'm a partner that is *TRUSTWORTHY!*"

Recite three times a day for five minutes daily.

In embarking on a journey of self-discovery to live one's purpose, relationships serve as the windows through which we gain insight into our strengths, weaknesses, and, ultimately, our purpose. We are challenged and tested within the realm of relationships, where our true character is revealed. Through the mirror of connection, we can see our strengths shine brightly as they are reflected in us by our partners. Conversely, our weaknesses are also exposed, offering us opportunities for growth and self-improvement. Moreover, relationships act as a compass, guiding us toward our purpose by providing valuable lessons  *and experiences that shape and define us. They offer a mirror into our souls, allowing us to recognize the passions and desires that drive us, ultimately leading us closer to living a life of purpose.*

Trust The Process

WARNING:

A PARTNER IS REQUIRED!

DO NOT START THIS PROCESS WITHOUT A PARTNER. IN ANY ENDEAVOR, WHETHER PERSONAL OR PROFESSIONAL, THE POWER OF COLLABORATION AND WORKING TOGETHER CANNOT BE OVERSTATED.

NO PHYSICAL CONTACT IS ALLOWED DURING THIS JOURNEY WITH YOUR PARTNER UNLESS YOU ARE ALREADY IN A MONOGAMOUS RELATIONSHIP WITH YOUR PARTNER. THE PARTNERSHIP IS STRICTLY A PLATONIC RELATIONSHIP DESIGNED TO HELP YOU EXPLORE THE CHANGES YOU NEED TO MAKE AND ACHIEVE SELF-AWARENESS. WHEN PARTNERS FOCUS ON THEIR CONNECTION BEYOND THE PHYSICAL REALM, THEY CAN NAVIGATE CHALLENGES TOGETHER, CELEBRATE ACHIEVEMENTS, AND ULTIMATELY FIND FULFILLMENT IN THEIR PARTNERSHIP. THIS INTENTIONAL DESIGN ALLOWS PARTNERS TO DELVE DEEPER INTO THEMSELVES, IDENTIFYING AREAS FOR PERSONAL DEVELOPMENT AND TRANSFORMATION. THUS, THROUGH THIS PLATONIC RELATIONSHIP, YOU CAN TRULY EXPLORE YOUR PURPOSE.

In This Partnership

"Announce Your Intentions"

My mother had a sign hanging over her bed that read, "Announce Your Intentions." I loved that sign because it permitted me to be transparent in a safe place with her. It also allowed for vulnerability, creating sacred conversations I treasure today. *Creating a sacred space is the intention of the exercise below.*

Before you start this exercise, cleanse the space-

Pray and ask God to cleanse the space. It is a powerful practice in spiritual partnerships. By acknowledging the presence of a higher power and inviting divine energy into the space, we create an environment that is purified and receptive to our intentions. This act of seeking spiritual cleansing allows us to release any negative energies or obstacles that may hinder the manifestation of our purpose. It also serves as a reminder that we are not alone in our journey but are supported by a higher force that guides and protects us. By starting our intentions with this sacred ritual, we set the stage for a harmonious and purposeful partnership infused with divine blessings.

Announce Your Intentions
With ENTHUSIASM and VIGOR

Announcing your intentions with enthusiasm and vigor becomes essential in pursuing your purpose. It calls us to wholeheartedly embrace our desires and aspirations, allowing them to resonate within us and guide our actions. By being passionate and releasing your intentions into the world, you create a powerful energy that reverberates, igniting a fire within you.

This vocalization serves as a declaration to us Sand the Divine, amplifying our commitment to our life path. Through this bold expression, we can feel the depth of our intentions enveloping us, propelling us forward on our spiritual journey.

Trust The Process

Exercise: Partners

"Announce Your Intentions"

Consistently announcing our intentions and discussing solutions to barriers we face creates an energetic ripple that creates opportunities for us to find ways to live our purpose. Practicing announcing your intentions daily and watching them transpire reinforces our belief in the power of declaring your intentions. In this daily ritual, we connect with our purpose. Below, answer the questions and share your answers with your partner in week two.

1. What is your life purpose? Do you know?

_____

_____

2. What *fears and barriers prevent you from achieving your purpose?*

_____

_____

3. What steps do you need to take to overcome these fears?

_____

_____

4. List three goals you hope to achieve.

    1. _____

    2. _____

    3. _____

Announcing one's intentions before embarking on a transformative journey of self-discovery is essential to living one's purpose. By openly declaring our intentions, we hold ourselves accountable and create a sense of commitment and focus. This announcement is a powerful reminder of our dedication to uncovering our true selves and living purposeful lives. It sets the tone for the entire journey. By sharing our intentions with others, we invite support and encouragement, creating a network of people who can provide guidance and motivation along the way. By answering these questions honestly and wholeheartedly, you will embark on this journey with clear intentions and an unwavering commitment to living your purpose.

Partnership Rules

Partnership rules are essential in guiding individuals toward walking on their purposeful path. These rules establish a framework for collaboration, ensuring that individuals work together effectively towards a common goal. By setting clear expectations and boundaries, *partnership rules* foster trust, respect, and accountability among all parties involved. Ultimately, these rules serve as a roadmap for successful partnerships, enabling individuals to navigate their purposeful path with clarity and unity.

Partners review the eight (8) essential *partnership rules*. Each partner will create rules 9 and 10 together.

1. Respect yourself and your partner
2. No drugs or alcohol during this journey - unless prescribed by a doctor.
3. Keep Your Word
4. Trust yourself and your partner
5. Commitment to this process 100%
6. Be accountable.
7. Celebrating Achievements and Milestones
8. No sexual relationship unless you are already in an intimate relationship.
9. _____
10. _____

Place initials below if you and your partner agree to these rules.

Partner (A)_____   Partner (B)_____

**By agreeing to these "Partnership Rules," you become accountable
to your partner, and two become one on this journey.**

Trust The Process

Before starting this exercise, "Announce Your Intentions" for this relationship. Decide who will be Partner A and who will be Partner B.

Partner A - answer the questions below. Partner B, please document Partner A's answer. Their answers provide valuable insights into who they will be along this journey. When Partner A finishes answering the questions, it is Partner B's turn.

1. I am committed to being a partner who:

    _____

    _____

    _____

    _____

2. I am a partner who will:

    _____

    _____

    _____

    _____

3. I could sabotage this relationship by:

    _____

    _____

    _____

    _____

4. I think my partner might sabotage our relationship by:

    _____

    _____

    _____

    _____

5. You can count on me for:

    _____

    _____

    _____

    _____

Please share your answers with your partner once you have finished answering the questions.

Partner B, it is your turn to answer the questions below in your book, and your partner will document your answers in your book.

1. I am committed to being a partner who:

   _____

   _____

   _____

   _____

2. I am a partner who will:

   _____

   _____

   _____

   _____

3. I could sabotage this relationship by:

   _____

   _____

   _____

   _____

4. I think my partner might sabotage our relationship by:

   _____

   _____

   _____

   _____

5. You can count on me for:

   _____

   _____

   _____

   _____

Please share your answers with your partner once you have finished answering the questions.

Emotional Growth Curve

Partnerships indeed have a learning curve that can be both challenging and rewarding. When individuals come together, personally or professionally, they bring their habits, beliefs, attitudes, and truths. These traits can lead to initial misunderstandings and conflicts as partners navigate this process of understanding each other's strengths, weaknesses, and communication styles. However, this learning curve allows partnerships to grow and evolve. Through open and honest communication, partners can learn from one another, adapt to each other's needs, and develop a deeper understanding of their shared goals. This learning process strengthens the partnership, enhances personal growth, and fosters a sense of emotional connection. Let's learn more about the "emotional" aspects of partnerships through the *"Emotional Growth Curve"* below.

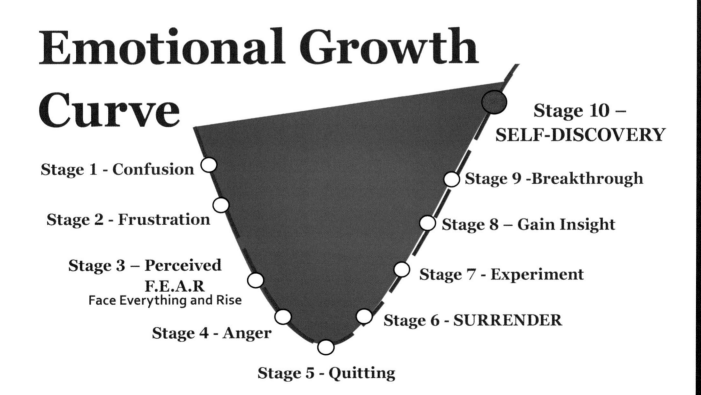

Emotional Growth Curve

Stage 1 - Confusion

Stage 2 - Frustration

Stage 3 – Perceived F.E.A.R
Face Everything and Rise

Stage 4 - Anger

Stage 5 - Quitting

Stage 6 - SURRENDER

Stage 7 - Experiment

Stage 8 – Gain Insight

Stage 9 - Breakthrough

Stage 10 – SELF-DISCOVERY

Trust The Process

Emotional Growth Curve

"Journey"

The "emotional growth curve journey" encompasses ten levels encapsulating confusion, frustration, perceived fear, anger, quitting, surrendering, experimenting, new insight, breakthrough, and self-discovery. Each level represents a distinct emotional state that individuals may experience as they grow. Confusion and frustration, these initial stages highlight the challenges and uncertainties that often accompany personal development. Moving through perceived fear and anger, individuals confront their insecurities and confrontational emotions. The subsequent stages of quitting and surrendering suggest moments of doubt and vulnerability that can arise during growth. However, in experimenting and gaining new insight, individuals explore alternative approaches and gain a deeper understanding of themselves. Lastly, the final two stages of breakthrough and self-discovery signify the transformative moments when individuals achieve profound clarity and knowledge about their true selves.

Overall, these ten levels toward "emotional growth" provide a valuable framework for comprehending the complex journey toward self-discovery to live one's purpose.

"History has thrust something upon us from which we cannot turn away."

By Dr. Martin Luther King, Jr.

Definition of "Emotional Growth Curve"

Stage 1:	**CONFUSION:** Our need for understanding and clarity.
Stage 2:	**FRUSTRATION:** Our inability to change something.
Stage 3:	**PERCEIVED FEAR:** Acronym Face Everything AND Rise
Stage 4:	**ANGER:** Feeling resentment and hostility towards something or someone.
Stage 5:	**QUITTING:** Abandoning something or someone. At times, people quit for an hour or years. *You are always choosing.*
Stage 6:	**SURRENDER:** Stop resisting what you cannot change.
Stage 7:	**EXPERIMENT:** Test hypothesis or new approach.
Stage 8:	**GAIN NEW INSIGHT:** A new understanding or comprehension.
Stage 9:	**BREAKTHROUGH:** Unexpected new awareness.
Stage 10:	**SELF-DISCOVERY:** Acquiring insight or knowledge into one's character.

The curve represents the bridge to self-discovery. If you get confused, frustrated, or afraid, know that you are on the path to a breakthrough, which leads to self-discovery. However, *red flags often precede a breakthrough*. These red flags are camouflaged to make you believe you have no power over your thoughts. But you do. Emotional ups and downs are part of this journey, and they represent new versions of yourself. So, talk it out and know that breakthrough is on the other side of these emotions!

Partners Commitment & Contractual Agreement

WARNING: Partners MUST Complete This Exercise Together

Please read and sign the contract below. Read the partner's contractual agreement and answer the questions below by checking whether or not you agree or disagree with the question. If you disagree, please openly and honestly discuss your disagreement with your partner.

1. Uphold confidentiality between partners –only share what your partner has permitted you to share.
    Agree ___ Disagree ___

2. Complete all exercises in the book.

3. Agree ___ Disagree ___

4. Follow all doctor-ordered prescribed medication you currently take per doctor's orders.
    Agree ___ Disagree ___

5. Do not enter a sexual relationship with anyone new.

6. Agree ___ Disagree ___

7. Promise to check in with your partner to cleanse and purge any conflict that could cause you to sabotage this journey.
    Agree ___ Disagree ___

You and your partner will sign the agreement below and begin week two.

Partner A - Sign Below and Date   Partner B - Sign Below and Date

_____   _____

Trust The Process

Shaken: The "Leap" Forward

Often, to *move forward* and make a great leap ahead, it is necessary to let go of certain things that may be holding us back. These could be negative habits, toxic relationships, or limiting beliefs hindering our growth potential. When we embark on a journey of self-improvement, it is inevitable that these aspects of our lives will be shaken, challenged, and ultimately left behind. However, it is essential to note that only some things can or should be discarded. Some elements of our past, such as cherished memories, valuable lessons learned, and essential core values, should remain steadfastly intact as we forge ahead. By recognizing the distinction between what should be let go and what should endure, we can navigate the path to a great leap forward with clarity and purpose.

Being "shaken" is not always a dramatic and loud event. It can be quiet, subtle, and required. Being shaken has a positive connotation if you think of it this way. These things include people and places that NEED to remove themselves from your space and put BEHIND you - will be. These people and places weigh you down and distract you from living your purpose. Being in their presence dramatically removes your focus from God and places your attention on things that do not matter as much as God's purpose in your life. These things and people hold you back from making a great leap forward.

Jesus, from the Gnostic Gospel of Thomas, said, "If you bring forth that which is within you, then that which is within you will be your salvation. If you do not bring forth that which is within you, then that which is within you will destroy you."

This process is much bigger than you and me, yet we both play an indispensable role in the bigger picture.

Hebrews 12:18 "shook or shaken" the removal of whatever is imperfect or sinful from heaven and earth."

Trust The Process

Exercise Shaken: The "Leap Forward"

What does the "leap" forward mean and look like for you?

_____

_____

_____

_____

_____

_____

_____

_____

_____

_____

_____

_____

_____

_____

_____

_____

_____

_____

_____

_____

_____

_____

_____

_____

_____

_____

Share your response with your partner.

A Story About Sisters Being "Shaken"

The Leap Forward

My sister Debra and I agreed to start a business in self-development in 2004. We held each other accountable for supporting each other to move the business forward. I am who I am because God put her in my life, and she is who she is because God put me in her life. The reason this partnership works is because of our phenomenal relationship. I am also a twin; we've been partners since conception. Because of Debra's fearlessness and confidence, I am fearless and confident. Her leadership and guidance have been a Godsend. My twin sister's partnership is a whole other level of partnership. Her heart is the best part of her, and I am honored to call her Twin.

I will forever be thankful to God for my sisters! Our seminars and workshops have benefited many people over the years. However, our business suffered at one point due to jealousy, resentment, distrust, insecurities, and lack of communication with my eldest sister, Debra. Truthfully, I was jealous of her talents and skills because they were different than mine. Debra had confidence, intuition, patience, and discernment, all the talents I had yet to develop. She also had a level of Faith in God I had never known up to this point. In my eyes, her abilities far exceeded anything I could achieve.

The more she shined, the more jealous I became. Until one day, Debra invited me to lunch at our favorite eatery. When I arrived, I noticed she was not alone; a new pastor she had recently met was sitting at the table with her. As I walked toward them, I smiled. I introduced myself as Debra's sister when I got to the table. The pastor and Debra stopped chatting and said, "Hello." I asked them if they had ordered any food. They said yes, so I ordered my favorite item on the menu. Then, while waiting for our food, the pastor shared with me why Debra asked her to attend this luncheon. As the pastor spoke, Debra did not make eye contact with me. I thought that was strange. Then, abruptly, the pastor said, *"Debra doesn't want to be in business with you anymore!"* She continued, *"Debra no longer wants to work with you because of your toxic attitude and sarcastic remarks during training."* I was devastated and appalled that someone I didn't know was telling me about my relationship with Debra. What shocked me the most was hearing this from the pastor and not Debra. Once the pastor made this announcement. I profusely refuted all her allegations. At that moment, I felt bullied.

So, I gathered my things and left! When I got in my car, I cried like a baby. When I finished crying, I heard a little voice say, "Is what the pastor said - right about me?" As I thought about the dates and times she referenced. My answer was a resounding Yes! It was my breakthrough moment, which was the moment that changed me and my sister's relationship forever.

At that moment, I said aloud, "She's right! I am jealous and resentful of her talents and skills. It was the most profound moment of my life because I was honest with myself for the first time. It was such a relief and embarrassment all at the same time. I immediately wanted to call her and ask for forgiveness. Later that evening, I called her and asked her to meet me to discuss our business future. She agreed, and we met two weeks later at her home. When I got there, we hugged immediately. Then, she offered me tea, and we sat down with each other. I felt her love, and she felt mine. The energy and passion in the room amplified respect and the fresh start we both wanted. Over time, we developed communication rules. The GOOD NEWS is that this process worked great. We built a trusting and loving relationship that grew into an appreciation for one another's talents and skills.

Being in a partnership has taught me that although we work together toward a common goal, we can still express our unique talents and qualities. The combination of our strengths has led to our success. Each of us brings our talents, skills, perspectives, and abilities to the table, adding value to the partnership and allowing for a more diverse and well-rounded approach to our business. This realization has helped me appreciate the importance of embracing my uniqueness without comparing myself to my sister, as it ultimately contributes to our business's overall growth and success. So that I never become jealous of my sister, we created partnership rules. These rules serve as a framework for open communication, trust, and mutual respect, allowing each individual to embrace their uniqueness while maintaining a solid bond. While it may seem counterintuitive to emphasize individuality within a partnership, a truly harmonious and fulfilling relationship can be achieved by recognizing each other's distinct qualities and a choice to *leap* forward.

A partnership is no place for jealousy and envy. In the journey of self-discovery to live one's purpose, partners must understand that jealousy and envy hold no position in fostering a healthy and productive partnership. While partners collaborate towards a shared objective, allowing negative emotions like jealousy and envy to seep into the dynamic can hinder growth and progress. Instead, partners should focus on supporting and uplifting each other, celebrating individual successes as collective victories. By cultivating an environment of trust, respect, and encouragement, partners can foster a strong bond that propels them forward on their journey of self-discovery and purpose.

Week Three:

DISCOVERING THE INFLUENCE OF UPBRINGING ON YOUR PURPOSE

Trust The Process

Section 2
Week Three:

Discovering the Influence of Upbringing On Your Purpose

"The number three represents harmony, WISDOM, and understanding."

Week three has a significant meaning. Biblically, the number three represents divine wholeness, completeness, and perfection. It represents the completion of a cycle or *the union of opposing forces to create something new.* The triad of mind, body, and spirit is another example of how three symbolize a holistic approach to spirituality. It represents the interconnectedness of individuals and their place within the world through their association with their mother, father, and themselves. Week three explores the influence of our upbringing and its impact on our purpose.

Week Three Permission Slip:

"I grant myself permission to UNCOVER AND APPRECIATE

how my parents or guardian prepared me for my purpose."

Recite three times a day for five minutes daily.

Family Support:

Families that encourage self-expression nurture our unique strengths, cultivate empathy and compassion, and enable us to explore diverse paths and discover our true calling. A family that values personal growth and encourages a strong work ethic instills the drive and determination to pursue our purpose with unwavering dedication.

Challenging Experiences:

Adversities faced during our upbringing can become catalysts for discovering our purpose. Challenges, such as financial difficulties, personal loss, or other setbacks, can shape our character and give rise to a heightened sensitivity to the suffering of others. These experiences often drive people to seek a purpose centered around helping others, making a difference, or creating positive change in their communities.

Role Models and Influential Figures:

The presence of influential figures in our lives dramatically contributes to the development of our purpose. Whether they are mentors, teachers, or community leaders, these people inspire us, impart wisdom, and provide valuable guidance. Their words and actions can ignite a spark within us, propelling us towards a purpose that aligns with their positive influence and the values they embody.

Trust The Process

How Our "Fixed Beliefs" Are Formed

Our lived experiences and influences indeed shape our *fixed beliefs.* Throughout our lives, we encounter various situations and interact with different individuals, each leaving an imprint on our thoughts and perspectives. Our experiences, whether positive or negative, contribute to the formation of fixed beliefs as they provide us with a frame of reference for understanding the world around us. Additionally, influences, such as family, friends, teachers, and media, significantly shape our beliefs. These external factors introduce us to different ideas, values, and ideologies that can either reinforce or challenge our existing beliefs.

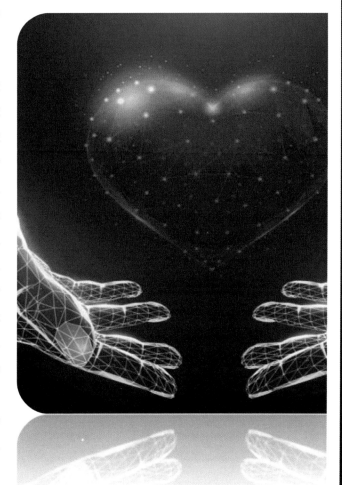

As babies, we enter a vast, complex environment that shapes our world understanding. While we may not have the cognitive ability to articulate our beliefs at such a young age, it is undeniable that we are actively forming a belief system from the moment we are born. Over time, these beliefs become fixed. Fixed beliefs can indeed have a significant impact on our relationships, both in negative and positive ways. On the one hand, when we hold rigid views about certain aspects of our lives, such as religion, politics, or even personal values, it can create barriers and hinder effective communication with others who may hold differing views. It can lead to conflicts, misunderstandings, and strained relationships. However, fixed beliefs can also positively influence our relationships by providing stability and shared understanding with like-minded individuals.

Trust The Process

The Four Attachments Styles:

The "Attachments" impact on partnerships.

The Four Attachments refer to four critical patterns of interaction that individuals may develop with their parents or guardians as children. John Bowlby, a British psychologist, and Mary Ainsworth, an American-Canadian developmental psychologist and an army veteran specializing in child psychology, created the four attachments in 1969. They agreed that knowing your attachments can significantly contribute to understanding relationships in the context of self-awareness. These four attachments play a crucial role in fostering emotional intelligence in a partnership by creating a secure and supportive environment for emotional expression and connection. By recognizing these attachment styles in yourself and your partner, one can gain insight into each other's emotional needs and behaviors.

The first attachment is the "secure" attachment style. A strong sense of trust and confidence in our relationships characterizes this attachment. Individuals with secure attachments tend to have healthy self-esteem, effective coping mechanisms, and the ability to form meaningful connections.

The second attachment style, known as "anxious" attachment, stems from experiences of inconsistency, neglect, or unpredictability in relationships. Individuals with anxious attachment often display clingy or dependent behavior, constantly seeking reassurance and fearing rejection. These individuals often struggle with self-doubt and anxiety and may face challenges forming and maintaining stable relationships.

The third attachment style, "avoidant" attachment, emerges from experiences of emotional isolation or neglect. Individuals with avoidant attachment tend to create emotional distance in relationships, often avoiding intimacy or vulnerability. They may have difficulty expressing emotions and forming deep connections, leading to a sense of detached independence.

The fourth attachment style is "disorganized" attachment, which arises from experiences of trauma or abuse. This attachment style often results in difficulties in trust, self-control, and forming secure connections. To effectively manage different attachment styles in a partnership, it is crucial to identify which one could represent you. Healing from the attachment is next.

Healing An Attachment Style

Healing an attachment style can be a transformative experience. It starts with reflecting on past experiences and noticing recurring themes or situations that consistently elicit negative emotions. Additionally, paying attention to physical cues such as increased heart rate or tension in the body can also indicate triggers. Once identified, developing coping mechanisms and strategies to manage these triggers is crucial. It involves seeking professional help, engaging in therapy or counseling, practicing mindfulness techniques, or engaging in self-care activities. Changing these triggers involves consciously reframing our thoughts and responses, challenging negative beliefs associated with painful childhood events, and replacing them with healthier, more positive perspectives. While this process may be challenging and require time and effort, it is possible to recognize and change triggers through self-reflection, support systems, and a commitment to forgive.

Forgiving others allows us to let go of resentment and anger, enabling us to move forward with a lighter heart and a clearer mind. Moreover, forgiveness also involves forgiving ourselves - for past mistakes and shortcomings, which is essential for self-acceptance and inner peace. By practicing forgiving ourselves and others, we allow the negative emotions and experiences that bind us to forge a new way of thinking about these experiences that come into our lives to teach us valuable lessons about ourselves.

Along This Journey

So, along this journey, *practice* **examining your behavior patterns and responses to challenging or emotional situations. Ask yourself, "Do I seek reassurance and validation from others? Or do I keep myself distant and avoid getting too close to people - so that I don't get hurt by them? Paying attention to your thoughts and feelings regarding intimacy, trust, and dependency toward others can provide valuable insights into your attachment style. Also, exploring your upbringing and early experiences with your parents or guardian can shed light on the origins of your attachment patterns. Understanding our attachment style can empower us to make conscious choices to be more communicative with our partners and work towards developing healthier relationships with ourselves and others.**

Trust The Process

Exercise: The Four Attachments

Identify the attachment below that best represents you by putting an (x) in the box. Please complete this exercise with your partner.

	Secure Attachment – They build relationships on trust and practice reliable - prompt, effective communication. They are always *emotionally* available for their partner.
	Anxious Attachment – They strongly desire closeness and intimacy in relationships, accompanied by a fear of rejection or abandonment. They constantly seek reassurance and validation from their partners and others, often feeling insecure and uncertain about the stability of their relationships.
	Avoidant Attachment - They often exhibit a fear of dependency and a strong desire for independence. People with an avoidant attachment may find it challenging to *trust others* and tend to suppress their emotions or emotionally detach themselves from others. They may also *struggle with expressing their needs and seeking support from others, as they fear rejection or abandonment.*
	Disorganized Attachment – They can showcase inconsistent and unpredictable behaviors. They struggle with regulating their emotions and have frequent mood swings. They often display contradictory reactions towards their partners, such as seeking comfort and suddenly avoiding or resisting their partner's attempts to soothe them. These individuals can be *aggressive or self-destructive,* exhibiting confusion and a lack of a coherent strategy for seeking comfort or safety.

Answer the FOUR questions below:

1. To avoid taking ownership of this attachment, *I could...*

_____

_____

_____

2. When I *read the traits* of this attachment, I felt...

_____

_____

_____

    a. The attachment I am *"fearful"* to reveal to myself and my partner is

_____

    Because it makes me feel...

_____

_____

The *benefit* of sharing these "attachments" with my partner

is..._____

_____

_____

Trust The Process

Starfish Analogy

The starfish analogy provides an insightful perspective on the four attachments. For example, like a starfish that clings to rocks or coral reefs, we too often find ourselves attached to various aspects of our lives. Let's pretend you are walking along the beach with your family, and you come upon a starfish. As you reach down to pick it up, your hand transforms into a starfish, and this same starfish leaps onto your face and becomes stuck there. The starfish represents your *"self-limiting beliefs"* that you have been walking around with your entire life. It impairs your vision and keeps you stuck in fear-based thoughts that handicap and restrict your view of what's possible for you. It even hides the solution, represented as your index finger on your opposite hand, pointing at you the whole time. All it takes to remove your starfish, or "self-limiting beliefs," is a willingness to remove your hand hiding your solution, represented by your index finger pointing at You. You are your solution.

Breaking free won't be easy because habitual habits and generational patterns prevent you from embracing a new "limitless belief" about what you can achieve. Remember, these negative behaviors did not start with you. They have been passed down from generation to generation. We inherited our parents' DNA that decided our eye color, how tall we would be, and behavioral patterns that created negative belief systems. We also inherit attitudes and addictive behaviors that produce destructive habits based on family genetics.

Exercise: The Starfish "Self-Limiting Beliefs" Got from My Environment

What "self-limiting" messages do you receive from your uncle, aunt, cousin, and other relatives?

_____

_____

What "self-limiting" message did you receive from your teachers, authority figures, and church members?

_____

_____

What "self-limiting" message did you get from your friends, neighbors, and society?

_____

_____

Family Pathology

Family pathology refers to studying and understanding dysfunctional patterns and behaviors within a family unit. It encompasses various psychological, emotional, and behavioral issues that may arise within the family system. Family pathology explores how these disturbances can impact the overall functioning and well-being of individuals within the family. It involves examining factors such as substance abuse, domestic violence, mental illness, communication breakdowns, and other negative dynamics that can disrupt family relationships' healthy development and functioning. By studying family pathology, researchers and professionals aim to identify underlying causes, patterns, and interventions that can help address and heal these issues within the family unit. It is not our objective to dive into anyone's family pathology. However, our goal is to provide insight into these dysfunctional patterns to our readers, motivating and encouraging you to learn more about these pathologies in your family dynamic.

Thanksgiving Dinner – The Family Pathology In Our Family

Several years ago, during "Thanksgiving dinner," my brothers broke out in a verbal assault on one another over a petty misunderstanding; it reminded me of the *disorganized attachments.* The way they attacked each other was seemingly out of the blue. Their disrespect for each other scared me because it reminded me of a story about a family member who killed their brother during a heated argument. The brother who survived is riddled with guilt and shame. I did not want that for my brothers or my family. So, I started crying and yelling, asking my brothers to PLEASE STOP FIGHTING! They did! Then, I reminded them how much I LOVED THEM. We hugged. I was relieved. They both apologized for upsetting me, and we hugged again tightly. I felt a shift in the room. A cycle was broken at this moment. I will forever be grateful for recognizing and interrupting their attachment pattern by speaking out with Love to my brothers.

It takes courage to speak out, teach, and educate the people you love about the four attachments. This education was the primary topic of our conversation during dinner that "Thanksgiving." I am so thankful to know the patterns of the four attachments. I am even more grateful that I can practice interrupting these patterns when they show up.

Exercise: What I Got from My Mother

What your mother gave you was **PERFECT** for you and your life purpose. Be gentle with yourself while completing this exercise, and go to a quiet place. After this exercise, discuss your answers with your partner and be transparent with them. *Focus on the qualities and talents you received from your mother, making you who you are today.*

IMAGINE YOUR MOTHER:

Describe her size, shape, skin color, eye color, hands, and feet.

_____

_____

What did she smell like?_____

What did her voice sound like?_____

What did I hate or dislike about my mother?_____

_____

_____

What did I love about my mother?

_____

_____

What did I want from my mother that I did not get?

_____

_____

What did I get from my mother that I did not want?

_____

_____

What did I resent about my mother?

_____

_____

What did I appreciate about my mother?

_____

_____

Trust The Process

Exercise:
What I Got from My Father

What your father gave you was **PERFECT** for you and your life purpose. Be gentle with yourself while completing this exercise, and go to a quiet place. After this exercise, discuss your answers with your partner and be transparent with them. *Focus on the qualities and talents you received from your father, making you who you are today.*

NOW, IMAGINE YOUR FATHER:

Describe his size, shape, skin color, eye color, hands, and feet.

_____

_____

What did he smell like? _____

What did his voice sound like? _____

What did I hate or dislike about my father? _____

_____

_____

What did I love about my father?

_____

_____

What did I want from my father that I did not get?

_____

_____

What did I get from my father that I did not want?

_____

_____

What did I resent about my father?

_____

_____

What did I appreciate about my father?

_____

_____

Trust The Process

Exercise: What I Got from My Family & Environment

1. What did your uncles, aunts, and cousins say about you?

_____

_____

2. What did your grandmother or grandfather say about you?

_____

_____

3. What did they say about your creativity, talents, and relationships?

_____

_____

4. What did your community, neighbors, and businesses in your environment say about you?

_____

_____

_____

5. What did teachers, coaches, and authority figures say about me?

_____

_____

_____

6. What did your place of worship (church) say about me?

_____

_____

_____

7. What did the news media and social media say about you?

_____

_____

_____

Based on your answers, which attachment styles could you be operating from? _____.

Identifying this attachment can help clarify what you need to change to improve your relationship with your partner, family, friends, and co-workers in the near future.

Trust The Process

Week Three: Weekly Reflection

"Your Life Story"

Everyone has a unique story that shapes their identity and experiences. It encompasses the various events, relationships, and milestones throughout one's lifetime. A life story is not just a chronological account of events but a reflection of the values, beliefs, and aspirations guiding an individual's actions and decisions. It is a way to make sense of one's past, present, and future, providing a framework for understanding oneself and relating to others. Internal factors, such as personality traits and desires, and external factors, such as family dynamics, cultural norms, and societal expectations, influence our life story. Throughout our lives, we embark on a profound journey filled with experiences, challenges, and personal growth. Only by actively engaging with *our life story* and making intentional choices can we discover our purpose and find fulfillment in it.

Please answer the questions below.

1. What *recurring themes or patterns* have emerged throughout your life story? *Reflect on the significant events and moments that have shaped you by focusing on the common threads that have consistently sparked your passion or interest.* _____

_____

_____

_____

_____

_____

_____

_____

_____

_____

_____

_____

_____

_____

_____

2. What milestones or turning points have profoundly impacted your perspective? *These can be personal achievements, challenges you overcome, or transformative experiences that have shaped your values and beliefs.* _____

_____

_____

_____

_____

_____

_____

_____

_____

_____

_____

3. What brings you the most incredible sense of fulfillment? *Examining the activities or pursuits that bring you joy and a sense of purpose, you can uncover important clues about what truly matters to You*!

_____

_____

_____

_____

_____

_____

_____

_____

_____

_____

_____

_____

_____

_____

By asking these three questions honestly, we can gain insights into our purpose
and how our life experiences have guided us towards it our entire lives.

Trust The Process

Week Four:

LISTENING TO GOD'S QUIET ANSWERS – "OUR ANCHOR"

Trust The Process

Section 2
Week Four:

Listening to God's Quiet Answers

"Our Anchor"

"The number four represents spiritual guidance, stability, and TRUST in God."

The number four holds significant spiritual connotations across various cultures and belief systems. Just as four walls and four legs on a chair provide stability and structure, the number four symbolizes a strong foundation in the spiritual realm. In the Bible, it represents "creations week." God completed the material universe on the fourth day, including the sun and moon. He said, "Let them serve as signs to mark sacred times, days, and years, and let them be light on the earth." (NIV Genesis 1:14-19.)

Week Four Permission Slip:

"God anchors me when I listen to His quiet answers."

Recite three times a day for five minutes daily.

Therefore, the fourth week of this journey represents a time to be grounded and anchored in a structure built to last in the physical world. In life's journey to live one's purpose, God serves as our anchor, providing guidance, wisdom, and support. This alignment not only provides us with a sense of fulfillment but also ensures that our actions are in line with His will. In the end, listening to God's answers allows us to **confidently** navigate life's challenges and uncertainties, knowing that we are following the path He has set before us. This week, listening to *God's Quiet Answers* for your life's purpose is the goal.

The Danger of PRETENDING to

Listen to God's Quiet Answers

Pretending to listen to God can be dangerous. Firstly, it can lead to a false sense of righteousness and moral superiority. When people pretend to listen to "God's Quiet Answers," they may adopt a holier-than-thou attitude, looking down upon those who do not share their beliefs. It can breed intolerance and division, hindering progress towards creating a new world based on unity and understanding. Secondly, pretending to listen to "God's Quiet Answers" can prevent genuine personal growth and self-reflection. By merely going through the motions without genuinely internalizing the teachings, people miss out on the transformative power of spirituality. This shallow approach can lead to a lack of empathy and an inability to connect with others on a deeper level. Lastly, pretending to listen to "God's Quiet Answers" may lead to manipulating others for personal gain. In essence, the dangers of pretending to have loyalty to God lie in the potential for arrogance, stagnation, and exploitation, all of which undermine the genuine pursuit of gaining knowledge and wisdom to live your purpose. Therefore, dedicating a week to actively listening for God's quiet answers can provide a sense of direction and stability we all seek. By anchoring ourselves in this listening practice, we align ourselves with God's divine plan for our lives, finding purpose and meaning in every step we take. Baba Ram Dass was an American spiritual teacher, psychologist, and author. His best-known book is titled **Be Here Now,** and one of his most famous quotes is, [2] **"The quieter you become, the more you can hear."** Another one of his favorite quotes is, **"The heart surrenders everything to the moment. The mind judges and holds back."** Thus, when we experience such positive, quiet, calm, and gentle knowing, we can be assured that God's voice leads us toward our purpose.

Why We Avoid - Listening to God

Avoiding listening to God can stem from various reasons. One of the primary causes may be the *fear of change or the discomfort of surrendering control.* Often, people find solace in maintaining their plans and desires, unwilling to acknowledge that a higher power may be guiding their lives. Additionally, *societal influences and distractions* can lead to a lack of attentiveness towards God's voice. It is essential to recognize these **barriers** and actively work towards overcoming them to embrace the anchor God can provide.

Here are three ways we avoid acting on God's Quiet Answers:

1. We *"pretend"* we don't hear what God asks us to do.
2. We *"practice"* working on things unrelated to what God is asking us to do.
3. We *"procrastinate"* on things God asked us to do.

God Woke Me Up at 4:38 AM

God woke me at 4:38 a.m. on September 16th, 2022, in Albuquerque, New Mexico. I was there to present a workshop on "Emotional Intelligence" to a group of leaders. I had been carrying around a notebook because God had given me quiet answers almost every day in 2022. When I awoke early that morning, I was excited to receive God's message because I had learned to recognize His voice, and I knew what He had for me would be phenomenal because I felt good that morning, and it was! God said, *"Lead, Teach, and Inspire people to Listen and Act – From Your Heart" to live their Divine Purpose."* Folks, it was a moment of profound significance when God gave me this message. In these moments, we are called to pause, reflect, and immediately act on God's revelation during these instances.

God's guidance serves as our compass, directing us toward the path that aligns with His will for our lives. We demonstrate our unwavering trust and faith in Him by heeding His quiet answers, which I did when writing this book.

What is God asking you to do - you have been avoiding?

_____
_____
_____
_____
_____
_____

What can you do to get in alignment?

_____
_____
_____
_____
_____
_____

Exercise: Elevate God's Presence

Elevating God's presence requires you to spend time in nature every day. When we open our heart space

during these moments of physical activity, we become more attuned to the beauty of God's creation that surrounds us in nature. Daily activity in nature heightened our awareness, allowing us to see the Divine in the simplest moments – a gentle breeze, a kind word, or even a serendipitous encounter. Practice the daily exercises below this week.

Day One: Mon	*Listen to beautiful music three times a day* - It evokes emotions, inspires reflection, and creates a sense of peace and serenity. When we immerse ourselves in the melodies and lyrics of a song, we open ourselves up to a realm where we can feel God's presence. Write down your "Quiet Answers" below. _____ _____
Day Two: Tues	*Go outside and walk in nature (one to two hours)* - It can evoke powerful emotions, inspire reflection, and create a sense of peace and serenity within you. In nature, we find a sanctuary and a tangible manifestation of God's presence, a constant reminder that *He is our anchor in life.* Write down your "Quiet Answers" below. _____ _____
Day Three: Wed	*Pray out loud three to five times throughout the day* - The act of vocalizing our prayers creates a profound sense of release as if the weight of our worries and fears is lifted from our shoulders. Write down your "Quiet Answers" below. _____ _____
Day Four: Thurs	*Write a letter to someone you love – Put pen to paper. See sample letters below.* Dear [Name], I hope this letter finds you in good health and spirits. As I write these words, I am reminded of my immense

love and gratitude for you. You have been a guiding light, a beacon of strength and unwavering support. You have celebrated with me in times of joy, and in moments of despair, you have held my hand and offered solace. Through your acceptance, I find the courage to face life's challenges head-on, knowing I am not alone. Through my faith, I recognize your presence as a divine gift. Your love has taught me the importance of compassion, forgiveness, and selflessness. It has shown me the power of empathy and understanding, allowing me to grow as an individual and deepen my relationships with others. Your presence in my life has indeed been a blessing, reminding me that even in the darkest times, there is always hope and love to hold onto.

As I conclude this letter, I want you to know that your love reminds me of the beauty in this world. Thank you for being the embodiment of love and the one I can always turn to. I am eternally grateful to you.

With all my love and admiration,

[Your Name]

Write down your "Quiet Answers" below.

_____

_____

Day Five: Fri	*Write a letter to your partner – Put pen to paper.*

Dear Partner,

I hope this letter finds you well and filled with the blessings of God. As I sit down to write to you, I am reflecting on our journey together. I have witnessed firsthand the power, love, and strength that comes from placing our faith in each other. You provide me with unwavering support, guidance, and comfort in times of uncertainty and doubt. Just as an anchor holds a ship steady amidst turbulent waters, you anchored us along this journey, providing stability amidst the storms we faced together. We encouraged each other to learn from our mistakes and face the habits that hold us back from our higher purpose. I will cherish this journey and our bond in partnership - for the rest of my life.

With love and faith, your partner for life!

[Your Name]

Write down your "Quiet Answers" below.

_____

_____

Week Four Reflection

"Elevate Your Awareness of God"

Introspection and reflection. Engaging in this exercise can deepen our understanding of the divine

presence in our lives. Please answer the following questions below honestly.

In what ways has God been an anchor in your life? Think about the moments when God supported, guided, and protected you. Share your answer with your partner.

_____

_____

_____

_____

_____

_____

_____

_____

How does your relationship with God shape your beliefs and values today? This question asks you to explore the impact of your faith on your moral compass, decision-making processes, and overall worldview. It allows you to acknowledge how your connection with God shapes your character and influences your interactions with others.

_____

_____

_____

_____

What practices or rituals help you feel close to God? Share with your partner.

_____

_____

_____

Trust The Process

Week Five

SELF-LOVE

IS "WHOLENESS!"

Trust The Process

Section 2
Week Five:

Self-Love is "Wholeness"

"The number five represents life changes, lessons, and the soul's purpose."

Number five holds significant spiritual symbolism as it represents change. The number five is associated with transformation, evolution, and growth throughout various spiritual traditions and belief systems. This notion of change is often linked to the five elements: earth, air, fire, water, and spirit, which are believed to be the fundamental building blocks of the human spirit. In numerology, five is considered a dynamic and energetic number that encourages individuals to embrace new experiences and adapt to different situations. Furthermore, in many cultures, the fifth chakra, also known as the throat chakra, is associated with communication and self-expression, ***highlighting the transformative power of words and ideas***. It can be concluded that number five is a spiritual reminder for people to embrace change and embark on personal growth and transformation to live their purpose.

Week Five Permission Slip:
"I give myself permission to mend the broken pieces within me by opening the door to self-love, self-acceptance, and self-growth!"
&
"I am worthy of ALL great things God has for me."
Recite three times a day for five minutes daily.

Self-love and "wholeness" are deeply rooted in our connection with God. Wholeness comes from a relationship with God, and His love is unconditional and limitless. In this love, we can find the strength to accept ourselves fully. Nothing or no one is separate in this space – we are all one. This connectedness heals all wounds, unites all countries, states, and cities, and empowers us. Our highest level of self-actualization can flourish in this place of PURE LOVE. God is the only source that raises our self-worth vibration and energy to "wholeness."

Self-love reminds us that we inherently deserve love, respect, and happiness. It reinforces the idea that our worth depends not on external validation or achievements but on our inherent value.

Trust The Process

Self-Love in Sisterhood

Sisterhood is an unstoppable force created to co-create with God and resonates deeply with me because of our connection to our spiritual essence. We have a powerful bond that uplifts and empowers others around us. The idea of being an unstoppable force speaks to the strength and resilience God built within us, which is the ONLY reason we can overcome obstacles and achieve greatness. Our collaboration enables us to tap into our unique talents and contribute meaningfully to the world. The transformative force empowers us to embrace our inherent worthiness and fulfill our purpose in partnering with God to fulfill our purpose. When my sister Debra, who helped me co-author this book, asked me what each week symbolizes, I was clear about each week except week six. When I didn't respond, she immediately said, "Week five should be about Self-Love." I panicked. When I heard those words come out of her mouth, I knew my self-love was extremely low – almost non-existent. Therefore, I felt like I was the last person who should be writing about self-love. My lack of self-love manifested in various ways, such as engaging in self-destructive behaviors - cutting my hair, eyebrows, and eyelashes whenever I felt insecure, settling for less than I deserved in relationships where my fiancé refused to set a date for our marriage, or career choices where the company I contracted with paid me below minimum wage.

Unfortunately, I knew my self-sabotaging behavior had firm roots in my childhood. The emotional bond formed during childhood was not extended to me by my father. There are several reasons this occurred. He is dead now, and we made peace with our relationship before he passed. As an adult, I sought validation and approval from others, constantly questioning my worthiness. The absence of emotional care in my formative years hindered my ability to establish a strong sense of self-worth, leaving me vulnerable to the opinions and judgments of others. It became apparent that I needed to address the wounds caused by the anxious-ambivalent attachment style. *This attachment style, characterized by a constant craving for emotional connection and reassurance, often leads to feelings of anxiety and insecurity.* Losing everything I held dear to me was the JOLT or DISRUPTION I needed to wake me up from my toxic behavior. Amidst my despair, I realized that my value should never solely depend on external factors or material possessions. This wake-up call taught me that true self-love comes from within. It drove me to embark on a journey of self-love, where I learned to value myself for who I am rather than what I have or who I was with.

P.U.R.E.

Perfect. Undeniable. Radiant. Evolution.
"That is, You!"

My experience reminded me of a friend who met a boy and fell in love. One year later, they moved in together. The relationship continued to grow, and she expected an engagement ring after four years of dating him. But no engagement ring came. So, she broke up with him, and what followed became the most incredible gift of all for her—a lesson in self-love. By leaving him, she *found her worth.*

In her process of healing, we created *PURE.* Pure is an acronym representing *Perfectly. Undeniable. Radiant. Evolution.* It symbolizes the transformative journey of self-discovery and self-worth. *Pure is a* powerful reminder when we embrace our imperfections and unique qualities that make us who we are, and it shines a light on our value. In these moments, we can call back our worth from wherever we left it. It is a powerful act of recovering our most sacred asset - ourselves. The lesson from these experiences was clear: When we allow others to define our worthiness based on their opinions or judgments, we give away our power and lose sight of our true selves. It is essential to recognize that our *Power* lies in our self-worth, and by calling back our self-worth, we take control of our narrative and, in doing so, refuse to let others dictate how we perceive ourselves. It is a courageous step towards self-acceptance and *self-love* that our soul needs to feel *worthy of all good things.*

My friend's experience and mine led to our greatest love - ourselves! It takes absolute courage to leave a toxic job or relationship. Our inner glow is the radiance or beacon that guides our journey to new heights of evolution. The Greek philosopher Aristotle described *self-love* as "One's love of something *'Kalon'* and good." Kalon means *seeing oneself as a magnificent creature - worthy of it all.* Only then can one exhibit *self-love.*" The only time I felt worthy of it all was in July 2021. It was the month I fell in love with Christ Jesus, and nothing has been the same since "Thank God."

Worthy – of it ALL

"Worthy of it all" speaks to the belief that everyone has value and should be treated with respect and dignity. Ultimately, it means living a life that reflects one's actual worth, which produces genuine fulfillment and happiness. Understanding the concept of being *"worthy of it all"* may require shifting your beliefs about yourself or others. Holding onto old thought patterns or habits prevents us from moving forward in new ways. To be *worthy of all*, one must challenge these negative beliefs and replace them with more empowering ones that honor the true nature of your worthiness. You have no idea how much your radiance or inner light is needed now. It is the source of motivation and inspiration for you and others. When you embrace your radiance, you embrace yourself.

Exercise:

Let Go of "NEGATIVE BELIEFS"

The exercise below involves acknowledging your inherent value by letting go of fixed beliefs that keep you stuck or broken. Answer the questions below and discuss your answers with your partner.

1. What does it mean to love yourself in a relationship?_____

_____

_____

_____

_____

2. What does **"worthy of it all"** mean to you in a relationship? _____

_____

_____

_____

_____

3. What would it look like every day in your life? _____

_____

_____

_____

_____

4. What does it mean to be a "magnificent creature?" _____

_____

_____

5. Complete these sentences:
    a. "I am worthy of _____
    b. "I am worthy of having a _____
    c. "I am worthy of living a life filled with _____

Trust The Process

Four Self-Love Exercises

1. The Power of Affirmations:

One powerful tool for daily self-love is the practice of affirmations. Individuals reciting affirmations reinforces self-worth and promotes a positive self-image. By incorporating affirmations into our daily routine, individuals can reprogram their subconscious mind, boosting their confidence and resilience and improving their overall well-being. Affirmations serve as powerful reminders of our worth and value. See the ten positive affirmations listed below that can aid in embracing yourself in this journey.

1. "I am worthy of love and respect."
2. "I choose to prioritize my well-being."
3. "I am enough just as I am."
4. "I deserve happiness and fulfillment."
5. "I forgive myself for past mistakes."
6. "I am deserving of love and kindness."
7. "I embrace my unique qualities and talents."
8. "I am proud of who I am becoming."
9. "I release all negative self-judgment."
10. "I am deserving of self-care and self-compassion."

2. Embracing Gratitude:

Expressing gratitude is another essential aspect of practicing self-love. Taking a few moments each day to acknowledge and appreciate the blessings and positive aspects of one's life can significantly impact mental and emotional well-being. Gratitude exercises could involve maintaining a gratitude journal, listing three things one feels thankful for daily, or expressing gratitude through meditation and prayer.

List three things you are grateful for:

1. _____
2. _____
3. _____

3. Prioritizing Self-Care:

Engaging in regular self-care activities is crucial for nurturing self-love. It can include daily exercise, adequate sleep, a balanced diet, and engaging in activities that bring joy and relaxation, such as reading, practicing hobbies, or spending time in nature. Prioritizing self-care helps individuals recharge their energy, reduce stress levels, and cultivate a healthy relationship with themselves.

4. Practicing Mindfulness:

Mindfulness exercises can significantly contribute to enhancing self-love. Mindfulness involves being fully present at the moment, without judgment or attachment. Daily mindfulness practices, such as meditation, deep breathing exercises, or mindful walking, allow individuals to cultivate self-awareness and acceptance of their thoughts, emotions, and physical sensations. This practice fosters a compassionate and non-judgmental attitude towards oneself, promoting self-love and inner peace.

Daily self-love exercises are essential for personal growth, well-being, and a fulfilling life. By incorporating self-affirmations, gratitude, self-care, and mindfulness practices into our routine, we empower ourselves to embrace our unique selves and nurture our overall well-being. Remember, self-love is a lifelong journey, and each step toward it brings us closer to leading a more fulfilling and authentic life.

Week Five Reflection

What is Your "Self-Love" Story?

Our self-worth story is a narrative that reflects our beliefs, experiences, and the way we see ourselves. For some, this story may be one of strength and confidence, where they recognize their inherent worthiness of love and happiness. However, for others, your journey of worthiness may just be beginning. Each person's self-worth story is unique; the key is to be honest and truthful.

_____

_____

_____

_____

_____

_____

_____

_____

_____

_____

_____

_____

_____

_____

_____

_____

_____

_____

_____

Week Six

NO MORE VICTIM STORY: <u>CHANGE IS</u> HERE!

Section 2
Week Six

No More Victim Story: Change Is Here

"The number "six" represents healing, love, support, and spiritual awakening."
The number six holds significant spiritual symbolism, representing healing, harmony, spiritual awakening, and the end of victim stories. In various spiritual traditions and belief systems, the number six is associated with the power to heal both physical and emotional wounds. It signifies letting go of past traumas through forgiveness, compassion, and love. This act releases oneself from the victim role. By embracing the energy of the number six, people are encouraged to take charge of their healing journey and reclaim their power by transcending their minds. By embracing the significance of six, we can achieve a sense of inner balance and alignment between our mind, body, and spirit.

Week Six Permission Slip
"I grant myself permission to CHALLENGE MY VICTIM story
by making it my PHENOMENAL story!"
Romans 8:28 says, "All things work together for good to those who love God and are called according to His purpose."
Recite three times a day for five minutes daily.

Challenges can be opportunities for personal growth and development. Reflecting on the story of my twin sister Cheryl and her group's assignment to make a difference in the world during a workshop, I am inspired by their proactive approach to creating positive change by providing a woman in another country with $25 to start a business. The only stipulation was that she had to pay it forward by giving three women $25.00 in a year or less. These three women would pay it forward by giving three other women $25.00. The massive difference these three women made that day" underscores the transformative power of partnership. Through such actions, we can break free from the victim mentality and recognize the power we possess through alliance.

This week, "No more victim stories" encompasses the notion that we can transform our challenges into opportunities by partnering with others. We can shift our mindset from victimhood to one of empowerment. This transformation is not a solitary journey; it requires partnering with people who can support us in rewriting our narratives. When we seek the guidance and collaboration of others, we can turn our victim stories into phenomenal tales of triumph and victory. Through partnership, we find the strength and inspiration to overcome obstacles and achieve greatness.

Trust The Process

What is a "Victim Story?"

A victim story is a narrative that people construct about themselves, often centered around their experiences of adversity, mistreatment, or injustice. It is a way of viewing oneself as a victim, where the focus is placed on external factors and circumstances that are believed to have hindered one's ability to succeed in a relationship or area in one's life. In a victim story, people attribute their hardships solely to factors beyond their control, leading to a sense of powerlessness and resignation. It is important to recognize that while acknowledging and processing past struggles is essential for healing, constantly dwelling on another person's actions against oneself can prevent us from taking responsibility for our actions and choices. Embracing a victim mentality can be detrimental as it hampers personal growth and hinders the ability to find purpose and fulfillment in the experience.

A victim story is usually about a relationship or situation that caused you pain, and you share this painful story with anyone and everyone who will listen. What makes it a victim story is how often the victim focuses on the relationship's pain or disappointing outcome. Here's the disclaimer: Some victim stories must be told because they help people learn from their painful mistakes. However, some people share their victim stories so often. They attract similar relationships that cause them the same pain because they refuse to learn the lesson previous experiences came to teach them.

I believe pain comes to change us. It's an indication that something within us needs changing. For example, my sister Debra, a single parent, suffered great pain and anguish raising a child with sickle cell. He was diagnosed with the disease at the age of two. I did my best to support her and my nephew. Our bond today reflects our lived experiences together. Our strength and devotion to the Divine taught us to trust Him through this painful experience. However, this experience developed our faith and a bond I cannot explain. *They are the two most "Amazing" people in my life, and I wouldn't be or have the confidence or strength without this experience.* Our story is **not** a "victim story." It is a victory, triumphant, and purpose-driven story.

Out of these challenges, we found our purpose. When faced with difficult circumstances, succumbing to victimhood and allowing our challenges to define us is easy. It is not easy shifting our perspective and embracing the notion that every obstacle presents a chance for self-improvement. This process unlocks our true potential. *Through this lens*, we can view our challenges not as setbacks but as stepping stones toward discovering our purpose in life. By embracing the lessons learned from these trials, we gain a deeper understanding of ourselves and the world around us, ultimately leading us to self-discovery of our purpose.

Trust The Process

Purging Your Pain:

Have you suffered the pain of a toxic, destructive, or broken relationship? Or have you suffered the pain of a lost family member, friend, or maybe a job? Has there been a heaviness surrounding you or an uncomfortable feeling of anguish, depression, and despair in your life lately? This week, you will be vindicated. What was meant for your harm, the Divine uses for your advantage? Past pain, anguish, sadness, or despair can heal – if you allow it. Let's talk about purging your pain. Purging our pain is a crucial step in walking on our purposeful path. Acknowledging and confronting pain requires deep self-reflection and introspection, as we must be willing to delve into our emotions and experiences to uncover the pain that comes to teach us valuable lessons.

Additionally, seeking support from your trusted partner or professional therapists along this journey can provide a safe space to express your pain and receive guidance. Engaging in healing practices such as meditation, journaling, or positive and safe creative outlets such as nature walks and moderate physical exercises can aid in purging our pain - if we also talk about it from a perspective of ownership. In most cases, *not all*. By actively facing our pain and our role in creating it, we can gradually release its grip on us, allowing us to move forward with clarity and resiliency. Purging our pain will enable us to shed the emotional baggage that holds us back, emerging stronger and wiser. Most relationships are in our lives for a season, reason, or a *lifetime,* and the ones for a season or reason have an expiration date. Our job is to learn and surrender to the season and reason. So that when a relationship comes into our life for a lifetime, we can sustain it because of the lessons we have learned in the season and reason relationships. So, when you think of the relationships or life situations that have hurt you the most, "THANK THEM - DON'T BLAME THEM," they played a significant role in your development if you learned the lesson it came to teach you. Every person on your path is there to teach you valuable lessons about yourself. You are on their path to teach them as well. But it's up to them to get their assignments. Your job is to get the lessons this person or situation came to make you aware of. So, please stop trying to make it about someone else when the experience comes to teach you a lesson. Accepting responsibility for your role in life's painful experiences will free and eliminate your victim mentality. Revealing the pain uncovers the change you need to make – **so don't resist it. Discover it – to learn from it**. Always remember if it doesn't challenge you - it doesn't change you.

"The thrust forward, the push toward change, renewal, and growth, is violently or stubbornly resisted by an equal will to maintain what is and has been." Don de Avila Jackson made this statement. He was an American psychiatrist best known for pioneering family therapy and founded the Palo Alto Mental Research Institute.

Prepare to Share Your "Victim Story?"

Preparing to share your "victim story" starts by planning to be honest, courageous, and transparent throughout the process. When it comes to sharing your victim story with your partner, it can be scary; preparation is essential—Start by considering the timing and setting in which you choose to share your story. Secondly, select a safe, private, and comfortable environment where both partners can openly communicate their emotions without others noticing. Thirdly, when you are ready to talk, go slow to speak clearly and concisely. Fourth, take it slow and easy by breathing in three to six deep breaths, and don't rush this process. Practice active and reflective listening. Also, show respect, appreciation, empathy, and compassion when hearing your partner's "victim story." By preparing yourself emotionally, mentally, and logistically, you can ensure that listening to your "victim story" will become a transformative experience that strengthens your bond and fosters growth for the listener and sharer.

WARNING

Sharing your "victim story" is not a time to be *passive, passive-aggressive, or aggressive.* It is a time to be *assertive by feeling and reflecting on what this experience came to teach you about yourself to move you forward.* Hence, proactive communication is necessary. It is a technique that involves expressing one's thoughts, feelings, and needs while respecting the rights and boundaries of others.

Respecting boundaries is crucial for each partner; actively listening and being attentive to your partner's verbal and non-verbal signals indicates your comfort level or desire for privacy. *Please discuss and showcase what each other's signs or cues look like when someone is crossing a boundary.* Also, discuss limitations when your partner makes snarky remarks about your story, which could undermine your experiences' validity and hinder any potential for growth and positive change. These remarks can generate a harsh, judgmental atmosphere, causing your partner to feel like you are dismissing or belittling their "victim story." So, be respectful and hold your verbal and non-verbal remarks for a time when your partner is ready to receive your feedback. *THIS PROCESS REQUIRES RESPECT AND SUPPORT.*

Trust The Process

Victim Story: No One-Size-Fits-All

"No one-size-fits-all" is a phrase that appropriately captures the essence of our "victim stories" and their impact on our lives. Each person's experiences, struggles, and triumphs are unique, shaping their narratives in distinct ways. Review these six steps before you share your "victim story."

Step One: *Who* – Your "victim story" is for your partner's ears only – **keep it confidential.**

Step Two: *What* – Share all of it, and don't leave anything out. Honesty releases *pain.*

Step Three: *When* – When you share, be well-rested.

Step Four: *Where* – Share your story in a quiet, private, and safe environment.

Step Five: *How* - Share your story in person, not on a virtual platform.

Step Six: *Give Your Partner the Benefit of the Doubt Regarding Their Story* – Believe their Story.

Before sharing your "victim story," "Announce Your Intentions."

Before you share your "victim story," announce your intentions by clarifying with your partner your intentions for sharing this story. The goal is to transform your "victim story" into a personal growth story filled with lessons and gratitude. By shifting your perspective, you grow from the experience.

Time to Share Your "Victim Story"

Next, decide who will be Partner A or Partner B. Partner A will share their "victim story" first, and then Partner B will share theirs. Partner B will listen and document their partner's story. Partner A will do the same when Partner B shares their story.

Writing or recording your partner's "victim story" can be a powerful tool in helping you stay focused on what your partner is sharing. **If you choose to record their story, please erase the recording immediately after sharing or sending the recording to your partner.** Recording your partner's victim story can indeed be a helpful tool in holding them accountable for the necessary changes they have agreed to make. Documenting their challenges and struggles, tracking their progress, and ensuring they actively work towards growth and improvement becomes easier. It also allows partners to reflect on the journey together, fostering a sense of shared responsibility and commitment to development—*time to share your story.*

How Did It Feel to Share Your "Victim Story"

Below, each partner will circle five words that describe how it felt to share your "victim story." Then, write them down and share why you selected these five words with your partner. **Write the five words you circled below. Share with your partner why you picked these words.**

1. _____ 2. _____ 3. _____ 4. _____ 5. _____

1) Anger	2) Embarrassed	3) Resentment	4) Depression	5) Guilt
6) Shameful	7) Unforgiveness	8) Uninspired	9) Hatred	10) Disgusted
11) Humiliated	12) Naked	13) Anxious	14) Confused	15) Denied
16) Anxiety	17) Nervous	18) Bitterness	19) Doubt	20) Exposed
21) Forgiveness	22) Calm	23) Graceful	24) Validated	25) Kindness
26) Brave	27) Heroic	28) Authentic	29) Happy	30) Respected
31) Humble	32) Daring	33) Heard	34) Anxious	35) Understood
36) Inspired	37) Courage	38) Valued	39) Empowering	40) Relieved

Reframing Your "Victim Story"

Reframing your "victim story" allows you to focus on the lessons learned, find strength in your experiences, and inspire others to do the same. See the "reframed" victim story sample below and practice reframing your victim story along this journey.

Sample: Reframed "Victim Story"

"One story that caused me immense pain was the sudden death of a loved one. Losing them was a devastating blow that shattered my world and left me feeling lost and broken. The pain I felt was indescribable. It was as if a part of me had been ripped away. It was difficult to navigate through the grief, as every aspect of my life seemed tainted by this profound loss. However, as time went on, I began to realize that this painful experience had the power to transform me in ways I never thought possible. Instead of being consumed by bitterness and sorrow, I saw this tragedy as an opportunity for growth and resilience. It pushed me to reevaluate my priorities, cherish the moments I have with loved ones, and appreciate the fragility of life. The painful experience taught me the importance of changing my "victim story" and finding the strength to see them as pathways for moving me forward in new ways.

Trust The Process

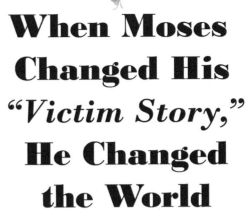

When Moses Changed His *"Victim Story,"* He Changed the World

Nothing about your life makes it clear that God has chosen you to change the world. But he has done just that. We are all here to shift the vibration and trajectory of these times, and God said, "I will be with you." From this perspective, we are very much like Moses. Moses escaped death by Pharaoh's hands, who ordered all the male babies to be killed because he worried the Israelites' young males would one day rise against him. So, Moses' mother sent him down the Nile River in a basket as a baby to escape this fate. What is mind-blowing is that Pharaoh's daughter, who was childless, found Moses floating in the river, picked him up, and raised him as her own. Moses, an Israelite, grew up as an Egyptian King under the very roof of the man who ordered him dead.

Isn't it funny how God will use unlikely situations and unlikely people to change the world? Your life doesn't need to make sense for God to use you to change the world, too. It can be messy and filled with holes, disappointments, confusion, suffering, frustration, and jagged edges, which makes it perfect for God. Your life is no more complicated, chaotic, or complex than Moses's, and God used him - just like he wants to use You.

Do you know what Moses' name means? According to Torah (Torah in Hebrew means God's revealing teaching), Moses comes from the Hebrew verb, meaning *"Draw out or Pulled out of the water."*

rocess

What does your name mean? My name, (Carolyn) means "Free (wo)man" and symbolizes inner strength and resilience. It represents "Spiritual Victory" on a quest for higher truth. Underneath her gentle nature lies a depth of inner wisdom and good character. My twin sister Cheryl's name means "Darling and Beloved," she is also living her purpose. Cheryl is lovely, beloved, and filled with an adoring nature for all people. My elder sister Debra's name is a feminine title of Hebrew origin. Debra is a biblical name born of a significant figure in the Bible of Judges. According to the Bible, Debra was a prophetess of God and the Israelites.

My sisters and I have Powerful names, and we are here to serve God in our purpose. Moses also became very powerful when he followed and listened to God. When Pharaoh's daughter drew him out of the water, she had no idea she was part of a *pre-destined plan to keep Moses alive to "Free" both his and God's people.* Many people forgot that Moses murdered a man, and yet he grew up as an Egyptian King. Moses did not have a foreshadowing of what his life would become. He could only become "Moses" by living a legacy of courage, determination, and tremendous bravery. His legacy cemented and circulated worldwide when he stepped into his God-given purpose.

Today, you can find the story of "Moses" in any biblical or religious book. Yet, what is not discussed is the Faith and Courage Moses needed to embrace, listen, and act on God's word. Moses's mother could never imagine that placing him in the Nile River would lead him on a journey of self-discovery and undertaking God's favor. His life appeared to be a fairytale because he was an Egyptian King, but that was just a cover.

Frequently, what is meant for our demise (Pharaoh's declaration to kill all male babies) turns out to be a daring and bold demonstration our enemy never saw coming. God reached down to rescue Moses, and the same God reached down to rescue us. Being rescued started a new chapter in his life, and the same is true for us.

Think about the daring and bold demonstration you made by taking this journey. Your *willingness tells God you are ready to be guided toward your purpose.* As you step out on faith and grow nearer to God, you will develop a knowing of your life's purpose. Your job is surrendering to it. When Moses was leading the flock on the far side of Horeb (The Mountain of God), he did not expect to find a burning Bush. Nor could Moses foresee conversing with the "Angel of God" while staring into the burning bush. But he did. What remarkable and holy experiences have you had with God? I have had plenty. They were glorious, and one provoked me to write this book.

Now is the time to stop holding yourself back. These turning points can change everything if we listen and act! Some of these experiences happen in the church at a worship service or during prayer. God is still with us no matter how stubborn or angry we get. God is the great "I am" that lives inside us; all we must do is embrace, listen, and act.

Week Six Reflection:

"No MORE VICTIM Story"

Week six exercises require time to reflect on why you might be hiding behind your "victim story" or making excuses for your inability to move forward in your purpose. Reflect and examine your conscious thoughts and feelings that pushed you towards a "victim story" that no longer suits you. Answer the questions below and spend some time reflecting on each one.

1. What disappointments in your lived experience or upbringing created this "victim story?"

   _____
   _____
   _____
   _____

2. How did these experiences impact your self-worth and self-esteem?

   _____
   _____
   _____
   _____

3. What pain or anger do you need to release?

   _____
   _____
   _____
   _____

4. How can you release this pain and anger?
   a. Here are some suggestions: 1. Identify the root causes of your pain; 2. Forgive the person for not being who you wanted them to be. It will liberate you from resentment and create space for personal growth. 3. Shift your perspective toward what you learned. These recommendations will aid you in empowering you toward personal growth.
   b. Share what you will do to release this pain below. Who do you need to forgive?

   _____
   _____
   _____
   _____

Trust The Process

Week Seven

THE POTTER'S WHEEL

Trust The Process

Section 2
Week Seven

The Potter's Wheel

*Number seven represents spiritual intuition, revelations, and BIG shifts -
that positively impacts your purpose.*

The number seven represents seven colors of the rainbow, seven chakras, seven days of the week, seven continents, and seven world wonders. In ancient Mesopotamia, each day of the week was associated with one of the seven celestial bodies visible to the naked eye - the Sun, Moon, Mars, Mercury, Jupiter, Venus, and Saturn. These heavenly bodies were believed to govern different aspects of life, and the number seven thus became associated with cosmic order and divinity. The number seven holds significant spiritual connotations in various cultures and belief systems. One of its spiritual meanings is closely tied to our purpose in life. In many traditions, the number seven symbolizes completeness and perfection. The statement that seven represents the potter's wheel and its ability to complete us holds a strong spiritual connotation.

In various religious and mystical traditions, seven is often associated with completeness, perfection, and divine harmony. Just as the potter's wheel shapes and molds clay into a finished vessel, the number seven symbolizes the transformative power that brings us to a state of wholeness. It represents the journey of self-discovery, divine harmony, and personal growth, where we undergo a process of refinement and purification.

Week Seven Permission Slip:
"I give myself permission to *DISCOVER MY PURPOSE.*"
Recite three times a day for five minutes this week.

Just as a lump of clay is shaped and molded by the potter's hands, we are shaped and developed through the trails we go through and overcome. The potter's wheel is where we are molded and transformed into who we are meant to be. On this wheel, we come face to face with our strengths, weaknesses, and hidden potential. On the wheel, we embrace our imperfections and uncover our true purpose. *The potter's wheel symbolizes the intricate dance between self-discovery and self-acceptance, reminding us that our character is not fixed but continuously evolving as we navigate the twists and turns of life. See below is the story of The Potter's Wheel illustrated through this "Teacup Story."*

The Teacup Story

A couple was visiting a teacup shop in southern California. As they admired the beautiful teacups, one of them suddenly spoke to them. It said, "I have not always been a teacup. At one time, I was a piece of red clay lying on the ground. Until one day, I was picked up off the ground, poked, prodded, and placed on a spinning wheel. Then, I was placed in a hot oven. I remember the temperature being so hot that I thought I would faint. Instead, I started yelling and screaming at the top of my lungs. Let me out! Let me out! But no one came to rescue me. Then abruptly, the oven door opened. What a relief. As I cooled off, no one could prepare me for what came next. Someone poured *paint* all over me, and it smelled terrible. The colors were beautiful, but the paint was sticky and smelly. Then suddenly, I was shoved back into the oven, but it was scorching hot this time. It felt twice as hot as before. Again, I BAMMED on the overdoor, yelling and screaming for someone to let me out! But, again, no one came to my rescue. This time, I knew I would suffocate and die, only that was when God stepped in. He was always with me, even when I was not with him. He asked me to grab a mirror, and as I held it up to my face, I could not believe my eyes. I said to myself, "I'm Beautiful!"

Ultimately, the teacup story reminds us that it is through facing and overcoming life's challenges that our true beauty materializes. During these trying times, our character is tested, and we have an opportunity to transform into the best version of ourselves.

What is Your Teacup Story?

Sample teacup story: *"My teacup story reflects my journey to discover my self-worth. Like a delicate teacup, I started feeling fragile and uncertain at a young age. Therefore, I was easily swayed by the opinions and judgments of others. I allowed external validation to define my worth, constantly seeking approval and recognition. However, when I lost everything dear to me, I realized that true self-worth cannot be found in the opinions of others. It lies within our hearts, where our souls reside. Just as a teacup holds the essence of the tea it contains, our hearts hold the essence of our soul's purpose.* ***Everyone has a teacup story.***

What is your teacup story?

How will you use your gifts and talents to serve the world?

_____

_____

_____

_____

_____

_____

_____

_____

_____

_____

_____

_____

_____

_____

_____

_____

What are you being built for?

_____

_____

_____

_____

_____

_____

The Teacup Exercise

Beginnings: Early childhood, first day on earth through kindergarten, ages 0-5.

Name some positive experiences.

1.

2.

3.

Name some challenging/negative experiences.

1.

2.

3.

Childhood: Preschool through elementary school, ages 5-10.

Name some positive experiences.

1.

2.

3.

Name some challenging/negative experiences.

1.

2.

3.

Adolescence: Awkward preteen years through high school, ages 10 to 19.

Name some positive experiences.

1.

2.

3.

Name some challenging/negative experiences.

1.

2.

3.

Trust The Process

Young Adult: To strike out independently, ages 19 to 25.

Name some positive experiences.

1.

2.

3.

Name some challenging/negative experiences.

1.

2.

3.

Adult to Current Age: adulthood is in full swing from the current stage of 25 to the present age.

Name some positive experiences.

1.

2.

3.

Name some challenging/negative experiences.

1.

2.

3.

Based on your life experience, positive and negative – what have you been shaped and refined to do?

_____

_____

_____

What are you PRETENDING NOT to know about your purpose?

_____

_____

_____

What is getting in the way of you pursuing your purpose?

_____

_____

_____

Trust The Process

Jonathan Livingston Seagull's

Teacup Story - Designed for His Purpose

Jonathan Livingston Seagull was a seagull who wanted to fly like the eagles. While other seagulls were content with their mundane existence of scavenging for food, Jonathan yearned for something more meaningful and fulfilling. He recognized that there was more to life than just conforming to societal expectations and limitations. Jonathan Livingston Seagull's parents believed that their purpose in life was to conform to the norms and expectations of their seagull community. They valued safety, security, and the simple pleasures of finding food and shelter. For them, life was about survival and blending in with the flock. Their beliefs were rooted in tradition and a fear of stepping outside the boundaries of what was considered normal.

Unlike his parents, Jonathan was driven by an insatiable desire to fly higher and faster than any of his kind. However, his relentless pursuit of excellence and non-conformity leads to the disapproval and rejection of his family, friends, and neighboring flock. As he faces the fear of being isolated and ostracized, Jonathan takes flight, and it is one of the most exhilarating and transformative moments of his life. As he soared through the skies, the overwhelming feeling of joy and fulfillment surpassed any previous sensation he had ever encountered. This transformative moment revealed Jonathan's passion for flying and gave him a profound sense of purpose. By pushing the boundaries and defying the limitations imposed upon seagulls, Jonathan discovered that his purpose lay in exploring his potential, pushing his limits, and encouraging others to do the same. This instance of pure bliss catalyzed Jonathan's quest to discover his true purpose in life and set him on a path of self-realization and enlightenment.

This book was published in 1970. Today, over 40 million copies have been sold worldwide. Most people don't know that several publishers rejected the book before it came to the attention of Eleanor Friede at Macmillan in 1969. *All it takes is one person to believe in you, and your life can change.* It starts with your desire and leads to your purpose.

Trust The Process

Aligning with your God-given Purpose

To live our purposes like Jonathan Livingston Seagull and countless others, we can begin by embracing risk-taking and leaving our comfort zone. In the next 30 days, challenge yourself to live your purpose by exploring opportunities to practice doing what God called ONLY you to do. This could involve pursuing a passion or interest you have always been curious about but have yet to dare yourself to do it. Living your purpose requires bravery, courage, and determination, so put 100% effort into it. Also, ENJOY every moment of this experience. That means NO FEAR ALLOWED.

Exercise: Practice Living Your Purpose

You are the only one who can answer these questions.

I will affirm myself daily for the next 30 days while I create a plan to live my purpose. The affirmations I plan to practice reciting are:

Example: I am Enough, I am Confident, etc.

I am _____, I am _____

I am_____, I am_____

The affirmations I created above will inspire me to live my purpose.

Complete the sentences below.

The talents and gifts I see in myself are _____, _____,

and _____. Using these gifts and talents will lead me to my purpose.

What I avoid that stops me from utilizing my talents and gifts is _____
_____

The reason I avoid this is because I _____
_____

What would happen if I stopped avoiding it? _____
_____
_____

Do you have a vision for your purpose? Write down the thing you can only do with God on your side. _____
_____
_____
_____
_____

To take steps toward your purpose, you MUST Give Yourself Permission to surrender and allow God to take over. How can you surrender to God? It is the only way He will take over your life.

_____

_____

_____

My purpose is to

To practice living your purpose, you will need the support of many people. List the top 5 below and how each one can support and help you.

1.

2.

3.

4.

5.

How did it feel to ask for support and help?

What are you learning about yourself and your purpose?

Carolyn would like to say "Thank You" for taking this journey!

Contact Information for Carolyn McCall:
For more information on how to reach Carolyn to discuss workshops, training,
and executive coaching, contact her at her website below.
Website: CarolynMcCall-Purpose.com

References

Don't Die with Your Music Still in You - PenguinRandomhouse.com. https://www.penguinrandomhouse.com/books/601292/dont-die-with-your-music-still-in-you-by-serena-j-dyer-and-dr-wayne-w-dyer/

≡Top 23 Self-Love Questions (+FREE Self-Love Resources). https://ineffableliving.com/self-love-questions/

DailyOM - Healing Trauma by Peter Levine. https://www.dailyom.com/cgi-bin/display/librarydisplay.cgi?lid=2018
Teacup story – author unknown

Like Clay in the Hand of the Potter | Christian Library. https://www.christianstudylibrary.org/article/clay-hand-potter
How do I change to transform my life? | Tony Robbins. https://www.tonyrobbins.com/stories/unleash-the-poIr/commit-to-change/
"The quieter you become, the more you can hear." - Goodreads. https://www.goodreads.com/quotes/49588-the-quieter-you-become-the-more-you-can-hear

Acts of Faith by Iyanla Vanzant - Ebook | Scribd. https://www.scribd.com/book/224416143/Acts-of-Faith-Meditations-For-People-of-Color

3 Ways to Keep Your Personal Life Private at Work - wikiHow. https://www.wikihow.com/Keep-Your-Personal-Life-Private-at-Work
http://www.healthyfoodhouse.com/jin-shin-jyutsu-finger-method-rub-certain-finger-60-seconds-see-will-happen-body/

Why do people say that all you have to do is believe in Jesus and you .... https://billygraham.org/answers/why-do-people-say-that-all-you-have-to-do-is-believe-in-jesus-and-youll-be-saved/

What is Healing? - Robin Hallett - Intuitive Healer & Light Sparkler. https://www.robinhallett.com/the-journey/what-is-intuitive-healing/

Inspiring Olympic Athletes - Some Examples. http://newsmanager.commpartners.com/tesolc/downloads/features/2021/Ancillary/2021-06_Cates_Appendix%20C.pdf

The Compass of Shame - Children of the Code. https://childrenofthecode.org/library/refs/compassofshame.htm

"The Former Factory Worker Who Predicted the Digital Age." The week, no. 1085, Dennis Publishing Ltd., Aug. 2016, p. 36.

Spiritual Renewal Bible New International Version, published 1998 Zondervan Corporation page 1302

90 Aristotle Quotes on Happiness & Life (EDUCATION). https://graciousquotes.com/aristotle/

"Lean not on your own understanding" – Proverbs 3:5-6 Explained | Faith …. https://faithisland.org/bible/lean-not-on-your-own-understanding-proverbs-35-6-explained/

Stanford Encyclopedia of Philosophy *First published Thu Sep 25, 2008; substantive revision Id Jul 29, 2015; and Biography Sep 10, 2019.*

How to Raise Your EQ Leadership Skill. https://www.linkedin.com/pulse/how-raise-your-eq-leadership-skill-maureen-ross-gemme-ms-ed-

Mental Health for Schools | LeapsForSchools.com. https://leapsforschools.com/mental-health-for-schools/

5 Intelligence II 5.1 THE EMOTIONAL INTELLIGENCE THEORY … https://courses.aiu.edu/BASIC%20PROCESSES%20OF%20THOUGHT/SEC%205/SEC%205%20BASIC.pdf

Who are the "experts" in emotional intelligence, and who …? https://www.eqi.org/experts.htm

History of Emotional Intelligence, Part Two | The Good Zone. https://www.thegoodzone.org/courses/1255131/lectures/27960509

11 Reasons to Give Therapy a Try in 2021–Black Female … https://www.blackfemaletherapists.com/11-reasons-to-give-therapy-a-try-in-2021/

NextGen Know-How: Beware of Compare | CU Management. https://www.cumanagement.com/articles/2021/06/nextgen-know-how-beware-compare

Walk, Run, or Bike Towards a New Life | Begin Again Institute. https://beginagaininstitute.com/blog/walk-run-or-bike-towards-a-new-life/

Trust The Process

An Inconvenient Beauty (Hawthorne House, #4) by Kristi Ann … https://www.goodreads.com/book/show/34020178-an-inconvenient-beauty

Mahoney, Ashley. "JCSU Needs All Hands on Deck to Make a Difference." The Charlotte Post, vol. 42, no. 25, Charlotte Post Publishing Co., Feb 23, 2017, p. 5A.

I hate my life and feel hopeless. https://www.positive-personal-growth.com/i-hate-my-life-and-feel-hopeless.html

What was your nickname as a child, and what did you do to …? https://www.reddit.com/r/AskReddit/comments/5hulx9/what_was_your_nickname_as_a_child_and_what_did/

Watkins, Leslie. "Dream BIG: FUNDING YOUR CTE PROGRAM TO MEET STUDENT AND PROGRAM NEEDS." Techniques, vol. 91, no. 5, Association for Career & Technical Education, May 2016, p. 28.

Dass, Ram, Baba. "Be Here Now" Oct 12, 1978 quote, "The quieter you become, the more you can hear.

Esther Friedman–Personal Development Coach–New York … https://www.yourtango.com/experts/estherfriedman

My Covid-19 Experience, Jun 4, 2021—Timmy Tae's Thoughts. https://timmytaes.com/2021/06/04/my-covid-19-experience-june-4-2021/

Wisdom Teeth Juneau AK, Dr. Charles J Schultz, Oral and … https://www.juneauoralsurgery.com/home-care/wisdom-teeth/

Carignani, Paolo. "'Psyche Is Extended': From Kant to Freud." International Journal of Psychoanalysis, vol. 99, no. 3, Taylor & Francis Ltd., June 2018, p. 665.

Uniting Our Suffering to Jesus to Find Healing–Healing … https://praymoreretreat.org/uniting-our-suffering-to-jesus-to-find-healing-healing-2019/

William Sunito, Author at Disciplined Entrepreneurship. https://www.d-eship.com/author/william-sunito/

Situational Depression—What It Is and What to Do About … https://www.bettersupport.com/advice/depression/situational-depression-what-it-is-and-what-to-do-about-it/

Rise Up … And Dare to Be Brave—Always Rise Blog. https://alwaysriseblog.wordpress.com/2018/03/23/rise-up-and-dare-to-be-brave/

How to Transform into Who You Want to Be. https://www.pyar.com/dating-tip/how-to-transform-into-who-you-really-want-to-be.html

360-degree feedback 360-degree feedback is one of the … https://www.coursehero.com/file/p3vgmgm/360-degree-feedback-The-360-degree-feedback-is-one-of-the-most-important/

The Church and Politics—Gospel Back in Politics. https://gospelnpolitics.wordpress.com/2017/10/17/the-church-and-politics/

Grant, Lynda. "Are You an Eagle or Chicken?" The Charlotte Post, vol. 40, no. 22, Charlotte Post Publishing Co., Feb 5, 2015, p. 3B.

Full article: Standing on the shoulders of giants … https://www.tandfonline.com/doi/full/10.1080/15294145.2020.1855938

Walk, Run, or Bike Towards a New Life | Begin Again Institute. https://beginagaininstitute.com/blog/walk-run-or-bike-towards-a-new-life/

Helton, Paul, G., and Stemler, Taraleigh (2021). *Released Overcoming Sexual Trauma Book* in Las Vegas, NV.

Rise Up … And Dare to Be Brave—Always Rise Blog. https://alwaysriseblog.wordpress.com/2018/03/23/rise-up-and-dare-to-be-brave/

Bach, Richard, and Bach-Parrish, Leslie, (1973), *Jonathan Livingston Seagull,* The Macmillan Publishing Co., Inc., New York, NY

Rodriguez, Adrian & Bowling, Alan. (2013). Study of the Stick-Slip Transition of Newton's Cradle with Friction. Proceedings of the ASME Design Engineering Technical Conference. 7. 10.1115/DETC2013-12420.

Once you find your calmness: you will never want to be … https://www.yoursoulfamily.com/once-you-find-your-calmness-you-will-never-want-to-be-without-it/

4.5. Compass of Shame | Defining Restorative | Restorative … https://www.iirp.edu/defining-restorative/compass-of-shame

self-awareness | Encyclopedia.com. https://www.encyclopedia.com/humanities/dictionaries-thesauruses-pictures-and-press-releases/self-awareness

How to Build Trust in Any Organization or Team • Chapman & Co. https://www.ccoleadership.com/resource/how-to-build-trust-in-any-organization-or-team/

Angel Figurine–Mother with Daughter–Reilly's Church … https://www.reillyschurchsup.com/angel-figurine-mother-with-daughter.html

Get Coding. by Young Rewired State—An In-depth Book … https://books-land.com/get-coding-book-review/

How to stop bleeding after a tooth extraction? https://www.dentistnewbury.co.uk/blog/how-to-stop-bleeding-after-tooth-extraction

Uniting Our Suffering to Jesus to Find Healing–Healing … https://praymoreretreat.org/uniting-our-suffering-to-jesus-to-find-healing-healing-2019/

Situational Depression—What It Is and What to Do About … https://www.bettersupport.com/advice/depression/situational-depression-what-it-is-and-what-to-do-about-it/

Zechariah 4:8 Then the word of the LORD came to me, saying, https://biblehub.com/zechariah/4-8.htm

Like Clay in the Hand of the Potter—NJOP. https://njop.org/like-clay-in-hand-of-potter/

Muir, Andrew. "Challenges, Changes and Motivation." Management Services, vol. 66, no. 1, Institute of Management Services, Apr. 2022, p. 4.

Joe Louis Quote: "A champion doesn't become a champion in the ring, he …. https://quotefancy.com/quote/1622300/Joe-Louis-A-champion-doesn-t-become-a-champion-in-the-ring-he-s-merely-recognized-in-the

"The quieter you become, the more you can hear." - Goodreads. https://www.goodreads.com/quotes/49588-the-quieter-you-become-the-more-you-can-hear

Quote by Alvin Toffler: "The illiterate of the 21st … - Goodreads. https://www.goodreads.com/quotes/8800-the-illiterate-of-the-21st-century-will-not-be-those

Matthew 5:16 In the same way, let your light shine before men, that .... https://biblehub.com/matthew/5-16.htm.

Proverbs 27:6 - Bible Hub. https://biblehub.com/proverbs/27-6.htm

Better Together: The 10 Ingredients Of Successful Partnerships - Forbes. https://www.forbes.com/sites/forbessanfranciscocouncil/2018/10/24/better-together-the-10-ingredients-of-successful-partnerships/

Romans 10:17 - Bible Hub. https://biblehub.com/romans/10-17.htm

NEFESH: The International Network of Orthodox Mental Health Professionals. https://nefesh.org/workshops/betrayaltraumahealing/login

Martin, J. (2018). Head and Shoulders Above. American Jails, 32(5), 77.

5 Ways to Practice Empathy in Your Relationship

https://www.brides.com/practice-empathy-in-relationship-6951684
"...Empathy? Empathy is the ability to understand and share another person's..."

Attachment Styles: Learn 5+ Valuable Things They Say ...

https://www.sandstonecare.com/blog/attachment-styles/
"...Secure attachment style Avoidant attachment style Disorganized attachment style Anxious attachment style Attachment styles...", "...Avoidant Attachment Style? Avoidant attachment style...", "...Attachment Style Avoidant Attachment Style Disorganized Attachment Style Secure Attachment Style...", "...Attachment Style? Anxious attachment styles, disorganized attachment styles, and avoidant attachment styles...", "...attachment style Avoidant attachment style Disorganized attachment style Anxious attachment style Attachment styles..."

Anxious Attachment Style: 13 Signs, Causes & How To Heal

https://www.parentingforbrain.com/anxious-attachment/
"...Secure attachment style Avoidant attachment style Anxious attachment style Fearful-avoidant attachment style...", "...attachment styles: Secure attachment style Avoidant attachment style...", "...attachment style Avoidant attachment style Anxious attachment style Fearful-avoidant attachment style..."

Attachment Theory: Bowlby & Ainsworth's Theory...

Trust The Process

https://www.simplypsychology.org/attachment.html

"...attachment theory in relationships? Attachment theory is a psychological theory developed by British psychologist John Bowlby..."

Disorganized Attachment Style: 7 Signs, Causes & How To...

https://www.parentingforbrain.com/disorganized-attachment/

"...attachment styles. Secure attachment style Avoidant attachment style Ambivalent attachment style..."

The 4 Attachment Styles: Which are you?

"...Secure Attachment Style The Healthiest Attachment Style People with a secure attachment style..."

Trust The Process

Printed in the United States
by Baker & Taylor Publisher Services